MEXICAN SOCIETY OF ANTHROPOLOGY, MEXICO CITY

On folded ⟨...⟩ *events and royal genealogies* ⟨...⟩ *uced in part here, read from b* ⟨...⟩ *d at Oxford University, begins in* A.D. *692 and ends abruptly in 1521, when Spain conquered the Mixtecs.*

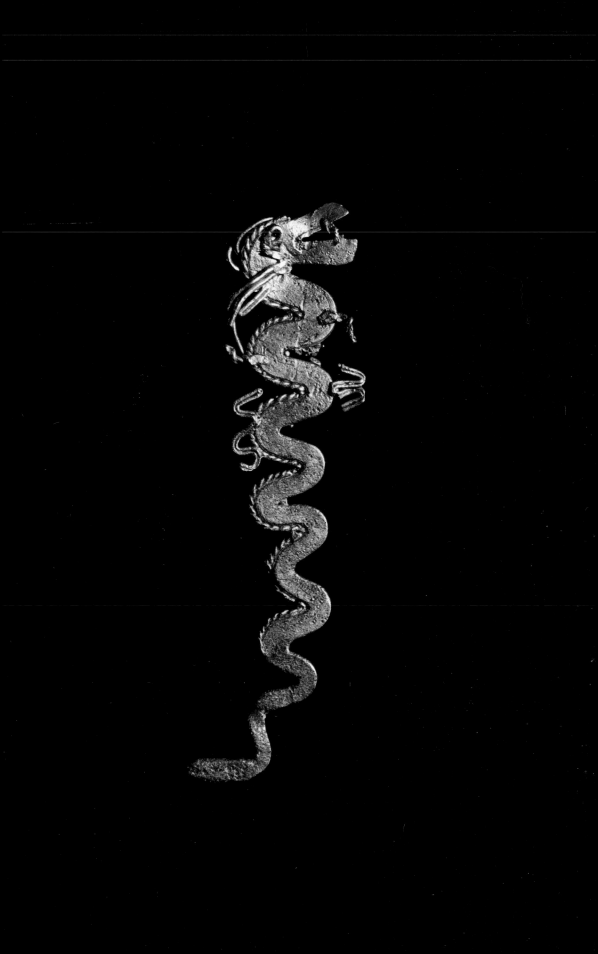

DISCOVERING
MAN'S PAST
IN THE AMERICAS

By George E. Stuart, *National Geographic Staff, and* Gene S. Stuart
Foreword by Matthew W. Stirling
Prepared by the Special Publications Division, Robert L. Breeden, *Chief*
National Geographic Society, Washington, D. C.

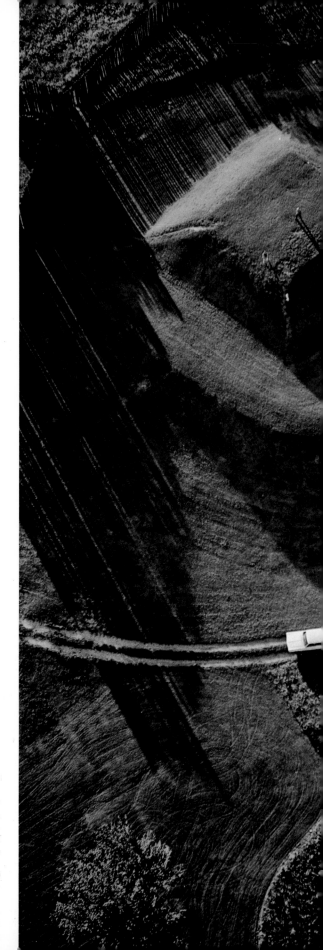

Discovering Man's Past
In the Americas
By George E. *and* Gene S. Stuart

Published by
The National Geographic Society
Melvin M. Payne, *President*
Melville Bell Grosvenor, *Editor-in-Chief*
Gilbert M. Grosvenor, *Editor*
Andrew H. Brown, *Consulting Editor*
Dr. Gordon R. Willey, *Consultant,*
  Bowditch Professor of Mexican and Central
  American Archaeology and Ethnology at
  Harvard University

Prepared by
The Special Publications Division
Robert L. Breeden, *Editor*
Donald J. Crump, *Associate Editor*
Philip B. Silcott, *Manuscript Editor*
Johanna G. Farren, *Research and Style*

Illustrations
Lowell J. Georgia, *Picture Editor*
Joseph A. Taney, *Art Director*
Josephine B. Bolt, *Assistant Art Director*
Penelope W. Springer, Peggy D.
  Winston, *Illustrations Research*
Margery G. Dunn, Ronald M. Fisher,
  Tadd Fisher, Mary Ann Harrell,
  H. Robert Morrison, *Picture Legends*
Virginia L. Baza, Betty Cloninger,
  Bobby G. Crockett, John D. Garst, Jr.,
  Map Research and Production

Production and Printing
Robert W. Messer, *Production Manager*
Ann H. Crouch, *Production Assistant*
James R. Whitney, John R. Metcalfe,
  Engraving and Printing

Suzanne J. Jacobson, Joan Perry, Carol
  R. Teachey, Sandra A. Turner,
  Barbara J. Walker, *Staff Assistants*
Dorothy M. Corson, Martha K.
  Hightower, *Index*

Revision Staff
Philip B. Silcott, *Editor;* Jan Nagel
  Clarkson, *Assistant to the Editor;* Marion
  K. Ingersoll, *Research;* David R. Bridge,
  Picture Editor; Ursula Perrin, *Design;*
  George V. White, *Production;* Margaret
  Murin Skekel, *Production Assistant;* John
  R. Metcalfe, *Engraving and Printing*

*Earthen platform that once held a ceremonial temple rises
within a reconstructed log stockade at Aztalan in Wisconsin, an Indian settlement dating from about A.D. 1000.
Overleaf: Artist's conception shows the central plaza of
Tenochtitlán, capital of the Aztec empire, as the Spanish
conquerors saw it in 1519. Page 1: Centuries-old gold-alloy
serpent of Colombia, just under 3 inches long, glistens in a
Bogotá museum. Book binding: Maya ball player dominates a representation of a stone disk on display in Mexico
City's National Museum of Anthropology.*

VICTOR R. BOSWELL, JR., N.G.S. STAFF (RIGHT); OVERLEAF: RICHARD
SCHLECHT; PAGE 1: LOREN MCINTYRE, GOLD MUSEUM, BOGOTA, COLOMBIA

FOREWORD

DURING THE MANY YEARS that I have been associated with the Smithsonian Institution and the National Geographic Society, I have been repeatedly impressed by the great popular interest in archeological subjects. Articles dealing with the science in the NATIONAL GEOGRAPHIC have invariably invoked an enthusiastic response from members, and the editors have received numerous requests urging that the Society produce a book dealing with the archeology of the New World. *Discovering Man's Past in the Americas* is the direct result of this expressed interest.

Archeology is, of course, the backward projection of the human story through interpretation of the material remains of past cultures. One of the remarkable things about this story is the unevenness of man's advance. While high civilizations developed and fell at widely scattered points, other large segments of humanity continued to exist at primitive levels. The anthropologist would like to know why. From the evidence of man's presence — artifacts, architectural remains, burials — the archeologist reconstructs the story.

In the Old World the archeological record of man goes back two million years and beyond, and involves the study of profound biologic changes which took place over this long period. In the New World the oldest firmly established evidences of man reach back only 12,000 years, although there is little doubt that the first scattered immigrants came much earlier.

These pioneer arrivals were nomadic hunters and gatherers. Not until 3500 B.C. was agriculture on a primitive basis established. By about 1200 B.C. we find the first sedentary civilization. There exists therefore in the New World a kind of controlled laboratory situation for studying the reasons for the rise of civilization, since there is considerable doubt that this development, or series of developments, was fundamentally affected by influences from across the oceans.

In this book authors George and Gene Stuart deal with the complex subject of American archeology both chronologically and regionally. The wide variation in cultural levels is made clear in descriptions of the simple hunting and gathering groups that existed throughout both continents, the semicivilized peoples of the southeastern and southwestern United States, up to the high civilizations of Middle America and western South America.

The human side of archeology, so rarely stressed in scientific monographs, is with us throughout the Stuarts' presentation. They have the facility of making the subject live, whether describing a mammoth kill or the majesty of a 200-foot-high Maya pyramid enveloped by the jungle.

Perhaps no general archeological account has ever been issued more up-to-date than this. As it goes to press it reports on a number of key discoveries by expeditions still in the field.

For those who may have thought of archeology as a "dead" subject, *Discovering Man's Past in the Americas* should be a revelation.

MATTHEW W. STIRLING, *Member, Committee for Research and Exploration of the National Geographic Society*

At Machu Picchu, in the Peruvian Andes, grass and weeds cover terraces where Inca India

CONTENTS

...ew crops centuries ago. Miles of such walled tiers changed the appearance of entire valleys.

1

A NEW WORLD

*Beyond their western ocean, Europeans find peoples whose
diversity and dazzling civilizations bespeak a long and complex past*

"WHAT IS PAST IS PROLOGUE," reads the inscription at the entrance to the
National Archives in Washington, D. C. I have often noticed it while
driving along Pennsylvania Avenue. Though the statement in this
instance refers only to our Nation's brief history, it applies equally to
the entire span of human life on earth; in order for us to understand
man's present—and to help guide his future—the knowledge and
lessons of this long past are essential.

Man's past can become a very personal thing. When I was a 12-year-
old in Camden, South Carolina, I paused one day at the window of an
antique shop where a display of arrowheads had caught my eye. At
that moment those bits of chipped stone became to me the most fascinating things in the world. Inside, I met the proprietor, Norman Fohl,
and asked their price.

"Not for sale," he answered cheerfully, "but do you have anything to
do for an hour or so?"

"No, not really," I replied.

"Let's go find some more, then. I know a field."

The field, about a mile out of town, lay on high ground near the Wateree River. I remember that the cotton had been picked, so that only
an occasional puff of dirty white remained on the dark stalks. A recent
rain had washed out the sandy rows. In the course of the afternoon
hunt—which stretched to four hours without my noticing—I picked

*New World metropolis, Teotihuacán reached its zenith in central Mexico
around A.D. 500. Beginning as nomadic hunters, the first Americans forged
great civilizations before Europeans arrived. The Taironas of Colombia,
fierce warriors and master artisans, shaped the gold chest ornament above.*

up hundreds of tiny fragments of Indian pottery and half a dozen arrowheads. We must have walked many miles, slowly searching up and down the rows, shifting direction now and then when we came across one another's footprints. For me the day opened up an exciting new world and began a lifelong friendship. It decided my future as an archeologist and predestined my four children, George, Gregg, Ann, and David, to grow up happily enraptured with American Indians and, of course, the remains of their dwelling places.

"What did that place look like before it was a ruin? What was it like to live there? Why did they choose that place to live?" And invariably, "Why can't we go there and see what it's like now?" Our older boys, George and Gregg, never seemed satisfied with the information we could give them, even about sites where we had worked. George, 13 and the oldest, had been too young to remember living in northern Georgia, where Gene and I spent several digging seasons at the Etowah Mounds, or being in Yucatán during the National Geographic Society-Tulane University excavations at Dzibilchaltún. Gregg had been born in Yucatán and cared for by a Maya nursemaid who ensured his success in life through the ancient *hetzmek* ceremony, in which she presented him with the basic tools of adulthood, among them a gun for hunting; a book, that he might learn to read; a coin, symbolizing money that he might earn to sustain his family; and a *coa,* a short curved blade for success in farming. Neither boy, though, had more than the barest recollection of this most unusual part of their lives.

The opportunity for Gene and me to relive these memorable personal moments—and to experience many more—came when the National Geographic Society assigned us to write this book. We were delighted when we realized that by taking the children along on some of our visits to New World archeological sites we could answer firsthand their questions about man's past.

We decided to begin our travels by visiting the Indian mounds on Mulberry Plantation near Camden, a site Mr. Fohl had taken me to some twenty years earlier. Soon, I knew, we would be seeing the ruins of spectacular stone cities in Middle America and the imposing cliff dwellings of our own Southwest, but first I wanted to take the children to a simpler site where man had lived out many lifetimes. Perhaps at Mulberry they could glimpse one facet of prehistory in the Americas, and thus better appreciate what they would see later.

In Camden we gathered at Norman Fohl's house and planned our short trip. It was summer, and Gene and I decided that the rigors of the South Carolina heat, the possibility of encountering snakes, and the long walk were not for the younger children, Ann and David.

Early next morning Mr. Fohl, George, Gregg, and I began the half-hour trek from the highway to the river's edge. A thick mantle of vegetation formed a nearly impenetrable fringe along the riverbank and the creek that joins it, covering the large mound so we could hardly make out its low shape atop the bank. As we pushed through brambles in an overgrown field, another mound appeared as a barely noticeable rise, just as I had remembered it.

I beckoned a very tired George and Gregg through the thicket near the mound, and the river appeared some twenty feet below. Cautiously we descended. The upper reaches of the escarpment, undercut and

.∴.Crow Flats

.∴.Fort Rock Cave

Danger Cave .∴.   .∴.Lindenmeier
                              Koster .∴.
Mesa Verde .∴.   .∴.Cahokia
Hawikuh .∴. •TAOS
           Pueblo Bonito
Snaketown .∴. Murray Springs   •ETOWAH
   Lehner .∴.   .∴.Poverty Point
   Naco .∴. .∴.Casas Grandes

                    Teotihuacán
TENOCHTITLÁN •   .∴.Chichén Itzá
      CHOLULA •
                      .∴.Tikal

• Sites inhabited in 1492

.∴. Sites abandoned by 1492

New World of 1492: Ancient living sites, crumbling ruins, and thriving cities dot the Americas at the dawn of European discovery. Radiocarbon dating of the ashes of Ice Age campfires reveals that man roamed the interior of North America at least as early as 10,000 B.C., and reached the tip of South America some 1,000 years later. Eventually great cities began to rise — and fall — in a continuing cycle that lasted until the coming of Columbus heralded the end of the dazzling Indian civilizations of the Americas.

MAP BY GEOGRAPHIC ART DIVISION

.∴.El Jobo

.∴.San Agustín
                              Marajó .∴.
Valdivia .∴.
Huaca Prieta .∴. CAJAMARCA
   Moche .∴. .∴. Chan Chan
   Huari .∴. .∴.Chavín de Huantar
Pikimachay .∴. •MACHU PICCHU
              •CUZCO
                .∴.Tiahuanaco

.∴.Fells Cave

11

draped with exposed roots, were as hard and as dry as concrete. The lower bank, a gentler slope of dark slime, was covered by a tangle of trees and brush that had fallen from above.

The Wateree River here loops toward the Mulberry site in a great meander that over the years has eaten into the large mound until much of the place has literally dissolved, its buried artifacts sinking beneath the water. Not all of them, though. Gregg, knee-deep in mud and precariously close to the stream, yelled to us.

"I found something!"

Slipping and sliding across the slope, the three of us joined him. Fatigue vanished as he washed his find in the river. It was a large fragment of shiny dark pottery with three lines incised upon it. Both boys suddenly realized that all the small humps in the mud hid other pieces. We collected pottery fragments all morning, then dined on canned beans in the cool shade of trees near the mound with the pottery spread out before us. Some of the pieces were incised like the first one Gregg found; some were plain. Others bore curved geometric designs stamped with a carved wooden paddle while the clay was soft, and a few of the rim pieces had rows of circles impressed with the end of a hollow cane. I explained that all the fragments were of a type of pottery found at sites in Georgia and North Carolina as well. They dated Mulberry's habitation to the 16th and 17th centuries.

AFTER LUNCH, Mr. Fohl and I showed George and Gregg the thick horizontal band of dark soil near the top of the bank and the layered cross-section of the mound that rose above. This portion of the site, not yet eroded by the river, we left undisturbed. The casual removal of pottery or charcoal there might erase forever some portion of our knowledge of Mulberry's past.

That night we thumbed through Mr. Fohl's copies of two old volumes published by the Smithsonian Institution in Washington, D. C. One, dated 1894, described the Mulberry site—then called McDowell—almost as we had seen it that morning, except that the large mound had been more complete and a third mound had been present. The other book, *Ancient Monuments of the Mississippi Valley*, printed almost 50 years before, contained an engraved map of the mounds around Camden as they had appeared in the 1840's. There had been ten mounds then, and an earth embankment had surrounded the site. Thus, as pages turned, the history of Mulberry passed like a film in reverse, but the story that unfolded was of a dead and deserted place. There had been no chronicler to give us even the smallest hint of what Mulberry was like as a living village.

There are accounts, though, written by the first Europeans to explore the Americas, that give us precious glimpses of other New World peoples and places in their last moments of cultural purity. One of the places we know from such chronicles is the Aztec capital Tenochtitlán, as Bernal Díaz del Castillo, a soldier of conquistador Hernán Cortés, saw it on an autumn morning 450 years ago. The little that remains of Tenochtitlán now lies beneath Mexico City. The six of us journeyed there to see a more grandiose facet of Indian life in the Americas.

We arrived at the end of October, when the mornings are chill, often with a low ragged haze in the earliest hours that soon lifts to reveal the silhouettes of the distant peaks and ridges that enclose the Valley of Mexico. On such a morning we stood atop Chapultepec, the small, rocky mountain that rises abruptly from the wooded park that bears the same name. Its summit is crowned by the National Museum of History, a castle of gray stone and arched doorways begun in 1783 as a home for the viceroys of New Spain.

In a way Chapultepec is a distillation of the long history of the city it overlooks, and of Mexico itself. Episodes of its past captured our interest in different ways. For three-year-old David, Chapultepec was an endless hall of flags and armor and gilt coaches. To Ann, eight, it was a place of gardens and wooded walkways centered upon a sumptuous palace for the golden-bearded idealist Maximilian and his bride Carlotta. For Gregg, ten and temporarily of military bent, Chapultepec was of still another era, some twenty years before Maximilian, when its plainer halls housed a branch of the Military College. It was late in the summer of 1847 when its cadets defended Chapultepec to the death against assaults by United States troops during the Mexican War. Rather than surrender, the last few survivors—the Boy Heroes—wrapped themselves in Mexican flags and leaped to their deaths. From the heights near where they died we looked eastward over the city.

A long segment of the Paseo de la Reforma, one of the most important of the modern city's avenues, drew our gaze in the general direction of Mexico City's central plaza. Half a turn to the right—and barely visible—the snow-mantled peaks of the volcanoes Iztaccíhuatl and Popocatépetl rode the distant horizon. Much closer, the Cerro de la Estrella, Mountain of the Star, rose at the near end of the hilly ridge that jutted toward us and encroached on the suburb of Ixtapalapa.

In the autumn of 1519 Chapultepec—Aztec for "Grasshopper Hill"—fronted on a great lake. Its summit held a religious shrine, its slopes and surroundings a tree-shaded park for the pleasure of Montezuma II.* Artisans had just added the Emperor's image to the sculptured portraits of earlier rulers that adorned the living rock at the base of the hill. Out from Chapultepec, Lake Texcoco covered nearly all the visible valley floor, and curved out of sight to form other lakes. About where the Paseo de la Reforma angles toward the center of the city, a stone causeway, with removable wooden bridges at intervals, led toward a wide, flat island some three miles away. Like thin white ribbons, other causeways reached to the same island, one from the north, another from the high ground near Ixtapalapa, then a lakeside town.

All the causeways met on the island at a walled religious area precisely where the central plaza is today. Visible there would have been the great pyramid topped by twin temples that marked the center of Tenochtitlán. From Chapultepec the city center would have appeared white as one's gaze passed from the large pyramids outward through the residential zones, the markets, and smaller temple clusters; then green on its fringes as the stone buildings thinned out and gave way to the agricultural plots that rimmed the island. These were the *chinampas*, or "floating gardens," that survive at Xochimilco, south of Mexico City—enormously fertile artificial islets of matted vegetation and mud held in place by the roots of transplanted trees. In all

---

*Many archeologists prefer "Moctezuma" to "Montezuma," the spelling used by Bernal Díaz del Castillo in his account of Cortés's expedition.

directions beyond lay the waters of the lake that nourished the chinampas and filled the canals that laced the capital.

The island metropolis was huge. Estimates of its population in 1519 run as high as 300,000—larger than the contemporary London of Henry VIII. The city must have appeared as an ornate centerpiece in the lake when the morning sun rose on the far side of the valley, and the scene was not hard for us to imagine: People thronged the causeways, some in the feathered headdress and richly embroidered mantles of the nobles, others in the coarse garb of the lower classes. White-clad figures manned long dugout canoes, guiding them toward the markets within the city, or to towns along the lake shore.

O N NOVEMBER 8, 1519, Tenochtitlán awakened to its last day of tranquillity—Hernán Cortés had entered the Valley of Mexico and was approaching from the southeast. Ten months had passed since the conquistadors' small fleet had rounded Yucatán, seven since it had landed on the Gulf Coast 200 miles east of the valley. The journey had been one of man's greatest adventures. Cortés and his small force had seen the stone cities of the Maya along the first coasts they sighted, and had skirmished with warriors clad in quilted cotton armor. Near the site of their final landing, they had visited the Totonacs at their capital Zempoala, a city of 30,000. It was here that Cortés had persuaded some 2,500 Totonacs to join his 608 men, for the coastal nation had recently been subjugated by Montezuma.

At Tlaxcala more Indians joined the growing army, and still more a little farther along at Cholula, where the conquerors looked in awe at the great pyramid that rose like a mountain above the temples. But nothing in their journey had prepared them for the experience of November 8. Bernal Díaz del Castillo recalled—in his 84th year—the wonder of the moment:

"In the morning we arrived at a broad Causeway, and continued our march towards Iztapalapa, and when we saw so many cities and villages built in the water and other great towns on dry land and that straight and level causeway . . . we were amazed and said it was like the enchantments . . . on account of the great towers and *cues* [temples] and buildings rising from the water. . . . And some of the soldiers even asked whether the things we saw were not a dream."

Thus did the Old World confront the New, if not in the first instance, certainly in the most dramatic. Norsemen had found their way to the western continent—had even established short-lived colonies—some five centuries earlier, but their saga passed into history with scarcely a ripple. More than two decades before, Columbus had come, but in all his four voyages he touched only the islands and forested coast that formed the outermost fringes of the new lands.

The essence of the drama played out beside Lake Texcoco lay in its being, in a sense, the first face-to-face meeting between the best of both worlds. In the long history of mankind the moment was without precedent, and its impact can never be repeated. The moment also bore the irrevocable seeds of tragedy, for after 1519 nothing could ever be the same. In the age of conquest that followed in the name of God and the greed for gold, one world would inevitably emerge the conqueror, the other the conquered.

As Cortés warily beheld the approach of the dazzling royal retinue from Tenochtitlán, and dismounted, holding a necklace of colored glass beads as a gift for the Emperor Montezuma, the rest of the New World lay virtually untouched. A land of formidable vastness, its two great continental masses each stretched some 3,000 miles from east to west. Together they spanned three-quarters of the distance from pole to pole and held one-fourth of the earth's habitable land.

Twenty-four hundred miles to the south of Montezuma's capital the Inca Empire, centered in Peru and rivaling that of the Aztecs in splendor, had reached its greatest extent. Twelve hundred miles north the scattered adobe villages of the corn-farming Pueblo Indians basked in the sun in what is now New Mexico and Arizona. Across the Gulf of Mexico lay the land discovered in 1513 by Juan Ponce de León, and named Florida. Covering all of what is now the southeastern United States, it was a vast unknown of woodland and swamp and small settlements, many of them dominated by thatched wooden temples set upon earthen pyramids. Just 13 years after Cortés entered Tenoch-

titlán, his countryman and distant relative, Francisco Pizarro, reached the town of Cajamarca in the highlands of Peru and began the bloody and deceitful conquest of that great New World civilization.

Twenty years later, in May 1539, the African adventurer and former slave, Estevan, entered the Zuñi pueblo of Hawikuh in New Mexico and died at the hands of its people as an unwelcome intruder. His companion, the Spanish friar Marcos de Niza, learning of Estevan's death, fled south, carrying the glowing but erroneous news of a settlement "larger than the city of Mexico." At almost the same time,

Hernando de Soto reached a small Florida village, where one of his chroniclers noted: "Their chief's house stood near the shore, upon a very high mount made by hand for defense"—the first mention of an Indian mound that has come down to us.

What these adventurers and others found in the first half of the 16th century were only small and random parts of the great world of humanity sheltered by the American continents. In the centuries of colonization that followed, more and more Europeans came upon seemingly countless other peoples with an astonishing variety of cultures and languages. But nowhere were there any real records of the great events, the gods, or the heroes. In their stead were enigmatic mounds, occasional monuments and silent temples, fragments of pottery, or simply the stone tools of early man; and these—like the living peoples of the Americas—were discovered largely by chance, their origins subjected briefly to fanciful speculations of lost tribes and sunken continents, and often forgotten.

Like the story of the Americas before Columbus, the story of more

In a detail from an idealized panorama painted on muslin, an Indian mound near Ferriday, Louisiana, discloses skeletons and burial offerings. Early in the 19th century antiquarians, treasure hunters, and a few serious students of man's past began opening many of the thousands of mounds scattered across the eastern United States. Some stood as simple defensive enclosures barren of artifacts, others as temple platforms or burial places.

than 99 percent of man's life on earth is unwritten. For gaining knowledge of this great portion of our heritage, archeology is indispensable. Its object is the recovery of information that an artifact, and what surrounds it, can yield for the understanding of our past. Briefly stated, archeology is the anthropology of extinct cultures.

The archeology of the New World, like that of the Old, has had its spectacular moments of discovery; these, however, are rare by-products of the science, infrequent but rewarding episodes in what is most often difficult and exacting work. It takes little imagination to share the thrill of the unparalleled discovery, in 1911, by Hiram Bingham. On a drizzly July morning he made the tortuous climb up the steep mountains along the Urubamba River in Peru's then-unmapped interior and found the city of Machu Picchu, much as the last Incas had left it centuries earlier. Recalling the first moments amid the vine-covered ruins, he wrote: "I climbed a marvelous great stairway of large granite blocks, walked along a *pampa* where the Indians had a small vegetable garden, and came into a little clearing. Here were the ruins of two of the finest structures I have ever seen in Peru. Not only were they made of selected blocks of beautifully grained white granite; their walls contained ashlars [hewn stones] of Cyclopean size, ten feet in length, and higher than a man. The sight held me spellbound."

Not as spectacular, but much more important in understanding man's progress, is the tiny charred cob of wild corn, the size of a kidney bean, that archeologist Richard S. MacNeish found in the 7,000-year-old zone of Coxcatlán Cave near Tehuacán, Mexico. The discovery, related to other plant remains in this and nearby caves, substituted hard evidence for years of speculation on the development of agriculture and the ultimate origins of high civilization in Middle America.

T HERE is no typical archeological site. One may represent the temporary camp of an Ice Age hunter, another the buried streets, crumbling temples, and refuse mounds of a great city. One site may be a cave, another a hilltop, and still another a stretch of land now uninhabitable, for climate and environment—as well as the ways of men—change through time. Each of these places, whether it be Mulberry, Tenochtitlán, Coxcatlán Cave, or Machu Picchu, is in a very real sense unique; each demands its own techniques of exploration. But each yields information that eventually gains it a place in the general sweep of man's long past.

In our travels we visited the sites of many of the great discoveries, and at other places we saw artifacts come to light for the first time. We watched archeologists in the field and in the laboratory, at work with shovel, trowel, and computer. We met scholars of the many other disciplines—geology, botany, linguistics, art history, to name but a few—that contribute knowledge vital in reconstructing past lifeways and human cultures from the evidence yielded by the ground.

Thus, research continues. As it does, and as techniques and scientific approaches are tested and refined, our picture of the unwritten past of man in the New World is constantly modified. So far, archeology has revealed more than 12,000 years of New World human history as complex and exciting as that of the Old World and of those Europeans who braved the unknown beyond their western ocean.

Morning sun burns away jungle mist in Mexico's Yucatán Peninsula. Vast areas of Middle America remain little changed since pre-Columbian civilizations flourished there. Uncounted ruins, cloaked by dense growth, await excavation.

GORDON W. GAHAN

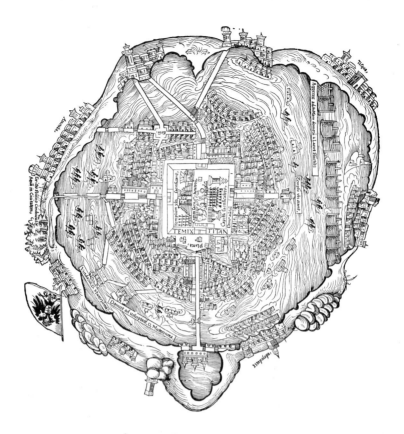

CONQUISTADOR HERNÁN CORTÉS AND THE AZTEC CITIES HE VANQUISHED

Slender causeways link the island city of Tenochtitlán, Aztec capital and present-day site of Mexico City, to the shores of Lake Texcoco. In 1519 Cortés marched on the city; its Emperor Montezuma II pondered whether the bearded conquistador was the god Quetzalcóatl returning from the east as prophesied; while he hesi- tated Cortés entered Tenochtitlán unopposed, after overthrowing the city of Cholula (opposite). There an archeologist excavates a burial. In the symbolic draw- ing below Cortés presents the New World to his sover- eign Charles V. Indians, some dressed in animal skins, pay homage. Banners implore the blessing of God.

Bright shawls across their shoulders, Indians from nearby hamlets bargain over produce—corn, beans, peaches, plantains, tomatoes—in Santiago Atitlán, Guatemala. Markets much like this fascinated 16th-century Spanish explorers.

JOHN M. KESHISHIAN, M.D.

A RUINED CITY REBORN

Restored tower rises above the Palace at Palenque in Mexico's Chiapas State. At left and above, workmen of the National Institute of Anthropology and History repair the structure's crumbling steps. The Temple of the Inscriptions, named for hieroglyphs carved inside on great stone panels, crowns the terraced pyramid beyond the hammer of the barefoot workman at left. During the seventh century a civilization of master architects—the Maya—reached one of its highest expressions here. Holding

22

RICHARD H. STEWART (BELOW) AND GORDON W. GAHAN

sway over the Yucatán Peninsula, the Maya developed ancient America's most sophisticated writing system, still only partly deciphered. Their astronomers translated the movements of the sun, moon, and Venus into mathematical cycles, using the concept of zero long before Europeans did. In the ninth century the Maya culture inexplicably began to decline; a hundred years later the remarkable civilization had virtually disintegrated. Encroaching vegetation choked the Palace in a 1942 photograph (right).

ARMANDO SALAS PORTUGAL (ABOVE) AND B. ANTHONY STEWART

GUARDIAN OF MEXICO'S HERITAGE: THE NATIONAL MUSEUM OF ANTHROPOLOGY

Huge umbrella of ribbed aluminum shelters the 600-foot-long central patio of the National Museum in Mexico City. A fountain drops a curtain of water around the single 40-foot pillar. Visitors stroll through halls rich with the relics of pre-Columbian Mexico. At left, sculptured relief duplicates that of the Temple of the Feathered Serpent in the ancient city of Teotihuacán, 25 miles northeast of Mexico City. Heads of the Feathered Serpent—the hero-god Quetzalcóatl—glare from a full-scale representation of the temple facade. A stone disk tops a goalpost from a ceremonial ball court. More than nine million people have toured the museum and its parklike setting since its opening in 1964. Scholars have access to thousands of volumes in the library and 12 million documents in archives. Mexican youngsters in a museum workshop practice the skills of their ancestors by fashioning clay copies of ancient artifacts. In a hall in the ethnographic section, photographs, paintings, and native crafts trace the course of Mexican culture from prehistoric times to the present.

GOLD'S PALE FIRE EVOKES
VANISHED CIVILIZATIONS

Reports by 16th-century explorers of vast treasure in the New World doomed the Indian civilizations. An early chronicler recorded that the Spanish conquistadors "thirsted mightily for gold; they stuffed themselves with it, and starved and lusted for it like pigs." Tons of irreplaceable artifacts reached Spain as ingots; some escaped destruction — buried in tombs or hidden away in temples. These Peruvian examples of the goldsmith's art span about 1,500 years.

At upper left, ringed by turquoise disks, a warrior of the militaristic Mochica culture stands poised with a spear-thrower on a fifth-century earspool such as he wears in his own pierced and distended lobes. Spiders on a 2,000-year-old nose ornament (lower left) weave a delicate web of braided gold. The figure opposite, possibly Naym-Lap, legendary 11th-century founder of the kingdom of Lambayeque on Peru's north coast, glowers from the handle of a ceremonial knife. On a 16th-century Inca gold relief — perhaps an armband (above) — felines, birds, and monkeys flank a mounted Spaniard. The steed's llama-like hoofs betray the Indians' unfamiliarity with horses.

LOFTY CITADEL OF THE INCAS

Lost to the outside world for nearly 350 years, Machu Picchu stands in ruined splendor in Peru, high in the Andes. Early in this century expeditions supported by the National Geographic Society and Yale University cleared the forest growth and rubble shown in this 1912 photograph to reveal the best preserved of all Inca cities. Expedition leader Hiram Bingham (right), his face blistered by exposure, found and photographed the site. Treasure hunters (left) search the Andes for salable remnants of their own past. Here, armed with rifles and machetes, they visit Bingham at Machu Picchu.

29

ARCHEOLOGISTS EMPLOY THE TOOLS OF THEIR TIME

In 1923 a Dodge touring car bogs down in a flash flood in New Mexico during the National Geographic Society's third expedition to the ancient Indian pueblos of the Southwest. At right, a helicopter airlifts supplies to a 1968 expedition excavating a thousand-year-old Indian settlement on the floor of the Grand Canyon. From the high Andes of Peru to Viking hearths in Newfoundland, the Society has supported the search for clues to the life of early man in the Americas. As times change, so do techniques. Archeologists of today detect ruins through aerial photography, probe them with sophisticated electronic sensors, and date them by methods ranging from tree-ring analysis to radiocarbon testing. Paleontologists, geologists, biologists, and specialists in scores of other fields may all work at a single dig.

2

THE BEGINNING

Man the hunter enters the Americas, adapts to varied environments,
and stands on the threshold of civilized life

"IT IS NOT LIKELY that there was another Noes Arke, by the which men might be transported into the Indies, and much lesse any Angell to carie the first man to this new world, holding him by the haire of the head.... I conclude then, that it is likely the first that came to the Indies was by shipwracke and tempest of wether."

This reflection by the 16th-century Spanish cleric José de Acosta was one attempt in the centuries that followed Columbus to account for the inhabitants of the Americas. Others ran the gamut of speculation from spontaneous generation out of mud to the Devil himself who, according to New England theologian Cotton Mather, "probably ... decoyed these miserable savages hither." In between, the ancestry of the American Indian was variously credited to Scandinavians and Egyptians, to Welshmen and Polynesians, to the Ten Lost Tribes of Israel, and even to Plato's fabled Atlantis. Acosta, however, had gone on to propose an Asian origin and had even theorized that the then-unexplored Bering Strait area was the crossing point.

Today, only 54 miles of water separate the tip of Alaska's Seward Peninsula from the eastern edge of Siberia, and between the two lie the shallows of their merged continental shelves. Around 24,000 B.C., in the final period of cold during the great glacial epoch, the Pleistocene, moisture evaporating from the sea fell as snow and formed a thick ice sheet that covered some of southeastern Alaska and most of

Dust of millenniums begrimes a student excavator at Murray Springs in Arizona, where spearmen slew a mammoth 11,000 years ago. Early hunters used tools like the stone knife above to butcher their kills. In game-scarce areas Indians gathered wild plants for food—and eventually began to farm.

SAM ABELL (OPPOSITE) AND N.G.S. PHOTOGRAPHER GEORGE F. MOBLEY

33

Canada. Eventually the sea level dropped several hundred feet, exposing the continental shelves and creating the Bering land bridge.

One night at home Gregg and I took a large map of the Western Hemisphere and traced on it the shorelines of North and South America as they might have appeared before the Ice Age glaciers finally began receding sometime after 8000 B.C. When we finished, both continents bulged outward slightly from their familiar map shapes, and a land bridge joined North America and Asia. Such was the geographic setting for the entry of man into the Americas.

The Bering land bridge seems a bridge only in relation to the tremendous size of the continental masses it connected. Actually it was so huge, as wide in places as the distance from the Great Lakes into Texas, that some archeologists refer to it as a subcontinent. To small bands of primitive Siberian hunters — unable to view it on a map as we had — Beringia must have seemed neither bridge nor link to another hemisphere, but only a continuation of their tundra hunting ground.

"They didn't even know they were migrating," archeologist Robert L. Humphrey told us during a morning visit in his office at The George Washington University in Washington, D. C. "They probably moved their campsites to coincide with feeding cycles of such game as the caribou and mammoth. As the animals slowly moved on, from feeding ground to feeding ground, the hunters followed. The rate of movement may have averaged no more than a few miles a generation."

TODAY, the upper limit of the boreal forest snakes out of northern Canada into Alaska, following the drainage of the Yukon River and its tributaries. The tundra of central Alaska — a land of standing water and tussocks of cotton grass, lichens, mosses, and bizarre miniature "forests" of birch and willow — accounts for most of the land north of the trees. On the polar seacoast beyond the Brooks Range lies Arctic tundra, a kind of far-northern prairie much as it was in the Ice Age, treeless and carpeted by reindeer moss that draws caribou in their annual migrations from one feeding spot to another.

At the peak of the Ice Age, with the land bridge and the tundra region free of glaciers east to the present Canadian border, Alaska was, in a sense, an extension of Siberia, and many of the early stone tools found there reflect this geographic continuity. Gravers, points, and knives from the Arctic coast and the Brooks Range resemble others found around Lake Baykal in central Siberia. The North American dates range anywhere from 16,000 to 6000 B.C., but these are only estimates. "The Arctic can often be an archeologist's nightmare," Bob Humphrey explained. "For one thing, the moist surface soil of the tundra 'creeps' over the hard, permanently frozen ground beneath, destroying all semblances of stratigraphy that could be used for the relative dating of artifacts. For another, on the Arctic slope, north of the Brooks Range, the growing season is so short that virtually no soil forms. This means that a stone tool, say 10,000 years old, might lie on the surface next to one dropped only a few centuries ago."

A rare exception to this geological trickery is Onion Portage, a site discovered by the late Brown University archeologist J. L. Giddings, Jr., in 1941. Onion Portage, named for the profusion of wild onions in the vicinity, lies within the constriction of a looping meander of the

Works of early New World artists, architects, and craftsmen reveal a complex story spanning more than 12,000 years of prehistory. This time chart relates the varied cultures as they developed within the Americas, from family groups banding together to hunt big game, through the beginnings of effective agriculture, to settled village life and the rise of urban centers. Old World highlights appear in the right-hand column.

A CHRONICLE OF AMERICAN PREHISTORY

MIDDLE AMERICA	THE SOUTHWEST	THE SOUTHEAST	SOUTH AMERICA	THE OLD WORLD

1500

Aztec Sun Stone, Mexico

Anasazi Mug, Wetherill Mesa, Colorado

Cedar Mask, Spiro, Oklahoma

Inca Wall, Cuzco, Peru

Conquistadors Embark for New World

1000

Toltec Warrior, Tula, Mexico

Mogollon Design, Mimbres Valley, New Mexico

Mississippian Temple Mound, Moundville, Alabama

Viking Era

Hohokam Palette, Snaketown, Arizona

Tiahuanaco Mirror, Peru

700

Maya Ball-court Marker, Mexico

Hopewell Mica Hand, Ohio

Fall of Rome

100
A.D.

Pyramid of the Moon, Teotihuacán, Mexico

Agriculture Established

Agriculture Established

Mochica Pottery Soldier, Peru

B.C.

Birth of Christ

Paracas Ceramic Arm, Peru

500

Colossal Olmec Head, Mexico

Adena Effigy Pipe, Ohio

Parthenon, Greece

1000

Stick Figure, Marble Canyon, Arizona

Adena Burial Mound, Ohio

Chavin Deity, Peru

2000

Grooved Whetstone, Russell Cave, Alabama

Agriculture Established

3000

Agriculture Established

The Sphinx and Pyramids at Giza, Egypt

5000

Clovis Point, North America

10,000

Hardaway Point, North Carolina

RICHARD SCHLECHT

Kobuk River, about a hundred miles inland from Alaska's west coast, and nearly on the tree line. Excavation there has revealed a veritable layer cake—20 feet thick in places—of Alaska's ancient history.

"The time span we have for the upper strata," Douglas Anderson, present excavator of Onion Portage, told me, "is now at least 9,000 years. The bottom levels could easily go back another 6,000."

At the lowest of more than 50 occupation levels lay large blades and other chipped tools resembling those shaped in central Siberia between 13,000 and 10,000 B.C. The top level contained outlines of Eskimo pit houses dating back only a few hundred years. Colored bands in between tell the story of the comings and goings of other peoples. Between 6200 and 6000 B.C. the occupants of Onion Portage were related to hunters of the Brooks Range to the northeast; afterward, the site lay deserted for some 2,000 years. By 4000 B.C. another group had arrived, apparently from the woodlands to the southeast, moving northwestward as warmer climate pushed their forest environment into what had been tundra. Around 2200 B.C. the cold returned to Onion Portage, and Arctic peoples again occupied the site, for the small delicate tools are those of a population called the Denbigh— probably direct ancestors of today's Eskimos—that flourished in the Arctic in the centuries after 2500 B.C.

The archeological importance of Onion Portage cannot be over-estimated, for with its well-defined stratigraphy it affords a unique opportunity for reliably dating isolated surface finds made in other areas of the barren land.

"I hope," Anderson added, "that further work at the site will take us back to the very beginnings of Arctic prehistory—with firm dates. What we've learned already, though, has helped clarify the sequence of events at the gateway to new lands."

The question of how many separate waves of people reached the Americas is yet uncertain. Indisputably there were at least two—one, the ancestors of the American Indians; the other, some time later, those of the Eskimos and Athapaskans. The physical diversity of the Indian has been accounted for in various ways. One theory attributes it mainly to separate crossings, another to gradual bodily adaptation to differing New World environments. Both undoubtedly played a part, but the picture is further complicated by "genetic drift"—the hereditary changes caused by the random isolation of small groups.

"Even more uncertain," Bob Humphrey told me, "is the time of man's first entry. So far, radiocarbon dating shows that people were well into the interior of North America by 10,000 B.C., and that by 9000 B.C. some had reached caves at the very tip of South America, 7,000 miles south of the Bering bridge. The first entry may have occurred as long ago as 40,000 B.C., as some collections of crude chopping tools and a number of disputed dates suggest."

Among these problematical sites, several on the fringes of the Valse-quillo Reservoir, southeast of Mexico City, suggest that man was there between 33,000 and 20,000 B.C. From Crow Flats in Canada's Yukon Territory, a caribou shinbone was recovered that had been fashioned into a serrated scraper. Its probable age has been determined at 27,000 years. At Lewisville, Texas, hearths yielded four radiocarbon readings that reached more than 37,000 years into the past, but the

RICHARD SCHLECHT

Stone projectile points, some grooved to fit arrow or spear shafts, appear in a profusion of shapes. A sampling of North American patterns, from bottom: Clovis, found throughout much of North America; Folsom, western Great Plains; the leaf-shaped Cascade, Pacific Northwest; Scottsbluff, Great Plains; and the Hardaway, North Carolina.

much later type of stone point found in one casts some doubt on this age. If the stone point was somehow introduced later, as archeologist Alex Krieger of the University of Washington, Seattle, thinks, Lewisville may yet prove "one of the most exciting and important archeological discoveries ever made in America."

In South America as well, the time of man's first arrival is confused by estimated dates or radiocarbon readings from Venezuela, northern Chile, Argentina, and Peru as early as 17,650 B.C.

The accessibility of interior America also bears on the question of the date of man's entry. Some geologists and archeologists believe that during the Ice Age, the grip of the cold relaxed from time to time; the melts opened an ice-free corridor that led from Alaska along the eastern margin of the Rocky Mountains. Other scientists hold that this corridor into what is now the United States was never completely blocked by glacial ice.

Whatever the final answers to the when and how of man's New World beginnings, the earliest culture that stands out clearly in the long continuum of his stay is that of the big-game hunters who roamed much of the United States between 10,000 and 8000 B.C.

O N AN EXPLORATION TRIP in the Southwest, my family and I crossed the Pecos River at Fort Sumner, New Mexico. It was there that the Navajo tribe spent its tragic four-year imprisonment before signing the 1868 treaty with the United States Government. Billy the Kid was killed there, too, and his grave lies on the outskirts of Fort Sumner. But our interest at the moment lay in the tableland beyond, for man had made it one of his early campgrounds.

The Llano Estacado, or Staked Plain, is a vast dry plateau that covers 20,000 square miles in eastern New Mexico and the Texas Panhandle. The high grassy plain slopes imperceptibly toward the east in an almost featureless monotony. Trees grow only along sandy stream beds or where man has planted them. Innumerable shallow depressions, or "blow-outs," pit the surface, scooped out by the wind.

Bone awl fits a grooved whetstone used by early inhabitants of Russell Cave, Alabama. Three National Geographic Society-Smithsonian Institution expeditions excavated the cave, unearthing evidence that man had lived there some 9,000 years ago. To preserve the site, the Society purchased it in the 1950's and in 1961 presented it to the Nation as an archeological monument.

Far-reaching effects of the Pleistocene glaciers made this a different sort of land around 10,000 B.C., cooler and watered by lakes and streams that nourished widespread savanna grasslands as well as stands of pine and spruce. Over this landscape roamed mammoths, camels, and bison, the latter somewhat larger than those the Europeans would discover much later on the Great Plains to the northeast. There were horses too, but these would eventually die off, along with the giant animals, as the glaciers withdrew and the climate slowly dried out over the next several thousand years. The horse would remain unknown in the New World until the coming of the Spaniards some 90 centuries later. Man also was here, and he hunted the big game with spears or short darts often tipped with fluted stone points. Such points—the Clovis and the later Folsom, both named for New Mexico towns near which they were first found—are among the hallmarks of the Ice Age hunters that archeologists collectively call Paleo-Indians.

These hunter bands spread rapidly throughout much of North America. Clovis points or fluted points closely resembling them have been found in nearly every part of the continental United States, in extreme southeastern Canada, and sporadically southward to Guatemala. The bands probably numbered no more than 30 people or so—about five families—who wandered separately, except during certain seasons when they might pool their resources for major hunting drives.

Positions of animal skeletons at Paleo-Indian kill sites provide some clues to what these hunts were like. At Dent, Colorado, near Denver, Clovis hunters apparently stampeded a mammoth herd over a steep bluff, then stunned the survivors with boulders and finished them off with spears. At the Lehner Ranch site in southern Arizona another sort of primitive ingenuity came into play. The nine skeletons found there with Clovis points were all of small immature mammoths, indicating that the hunters had separated the weaker animals from the herd. Most kills took place beside lakes or streams where animals were surprised as they watered, then killed as they panicked and became mired in the soft, moist ground.

Although the big-game hunts of the Paleo-Indians "imparted a design, a style to their lives," as Gordon R. Willey of Harvard University's Peabody Museum of Archaeology and Ethnology put it, hunting was by no means their sole activity. It is misleading to visualize these early people exclusively in recurring scenes of rearing, frightened animals surrounded by frantic, skin-clad spear-wielders. To emphasize this point, one archeologist remarked, "The man who bagged a mammoth probably spent the rest of his life talking about it."

At the Levi rock-shelter in central Texas, remains of big game were rare; instead there were bones of deer and of rabbits and small rodents. Stone implements at Levi, like those of the Shoop site in far-off Pennsylvania, ranged from specialized scrapers to pointed gravers, suggesting a variety of activities, perhaps including the manufacture of wooden implements. The abundance of hard, easily flaked chert at the Williamson site in southern Virginia, on the other hand, betrays it as a quarry station for the production of fluted points.

T HE PALEO-INDIAN CAMP discovered on the Lindenmeier Ranch in eastern Colorado in the 1930's gives a more complete picture of life shortly after 9000 B.C. "We have something like 20,000 artifacts from Lindenmeier, mostly stone blades and projectile points," Edwin N. Wilmsen told me when I visited his combined office-laboratory at the Smithsonian Institution. "The site has been extensively excavated at different times and the exact location of every piece carefully mapped," he continued, indicating large detail-filled wall charts. Shallow boxes and trays of numbered stone and bone tools covered long plywood tables.

Ed is measuring all the artifacts, noting the material of manufacture, and transferring the data to cards for computer analysis in the hope that the correlation of artifact variety with the location of each on the ancient living floors will increase our knowledge of life in such camps.

At the time man occupied the Lindenmeier site, the mammoths had begun to die off. For at least several generations, bands gathered there —probably in late summer or early fall—for communal hunts of bison, antelope, and deer. One part of the site holds the remains of a bison kill. In other areas large concentrations of unfinished Folsom points, as well as scrapers and chipping debris, bespeak much time spent in camp making and repairing the delicate points. Bone needles suggest

38

that the ancient campfires of Lindenmeier might well have revealed women working and sewing bison hides for clothing while others prepared the skins of newly butchered animals.

What did the Paleo-Indian hunter look like? Few of his bones have been found, and as yet none has dated from the Clovis period. In 1953, among dunes near Midland, Texas, wind exposed fragments of human bone and an unfluted Folsom point. Later, radiocarbon tests dated the bone around 8500 B.C. Physical anthropologist T. Dale Stewart of the Smithsonian Institution meticulously pieced together dozens of small skull fragments and revealed that "Midland Man" — really a woman about 30 years old — had a head markedly greater in length than in width. With the exception of round-headed Tepexpan Man — a skeleton unearthed near Mexico City, and believed by some archeologists to date from the Ice Age — the long shape characterizes the few other apparently early skull fragments found as far south as Brazil.

After 8000 B.C., the Ice Age came to a gradual end. The northern glaciers pulled back from the Great Lakes, and the large herd animals to the south, unable to cope with the fluctuation in their environment, began the slow move to extinction. In the Great Plains hunters continued to stalk bison, but the people of the eastern woodlands, deprived of the tree-browsing mastodon and other large herbivores, turned increasingly to fishing, the gathering of edible plants, and the hunting of smaller forest game. In a 7,000-year span the woodlands people developed a wide range of skills that gradually saw the introduction of a great variety of notched or stemmed projectile points, ground and polished stone artifacts including perforated spear-thrower weights, grooved ax heads, crude soapstone bowls, and ultimately — between 2000 and 1000 B.C. — clay pottery.

Gateway to the Americas, the Bering land bridge (light green) led nomadic hunters — through many generations — from present-day Siberia into Alaska. Successive eras of cold and warmth during the Ice Age alternately uncovered and drowned the swamp-laced tundra of the bridge. A final glacial melt, beginning after 8000 B.C., slowly raised the sea level, separating the continents.

The spear-thrower, or *atlatl*, as the Aztecs would name it much later, is, like most ingenious inventions, both simple and—with a little practice—very effective. Basically it is a stick about two feet long with a small hooked tip. Grasped in the hand, with a spear base set against the tip, it becomes an extension of the arm, allowing the thrower to propel the weapon with much greater force than the arm alone provides. We have two at home, bought in a curio shop in Mexico. With them George and Gregg quickly became proficient at hurling spears. Amazed at his newfound strength, Gregg exulted afterward, "It made me feel ten feet tall!"

Paleo-Indian hunters probably made good use of the atlatl, as did the later occupants of Russell Cave in northeastern Alabama. Excavations there, carried out by Smithsonian archeologist Carl F. Miller with the aid of a National Geographic Society research grant, showed one kind of eastern woodland life—that of the forest hunter and gatherer. Successive strata that reached back to about 7000 B.C., the very beginnings of the period called Archaic by archeologists, yielded the bones of deer, bears, raccoons, and turkeys, as well as wild plant foods.

Other sites in the Southeast reflect a different life—that of the shellfish eaters, whose large refuse heaps of discarded mussel shells mark such sites as Eva in northern Tennessee and uncounted others along the rivers and on the coastline from the Middle Atlantic states around the Florida peninsula to the mouth of the Mississippi.

Each of these site types may represent peoples with different livelihoods, or the life of a single group whose food pursuits varied with the seasons. According to a chronicle about the early backcountry North Carolina Indians, they "came regularly in the early springtime to the coast of the Cape Fear for the seawater fish and oysters which were abundant."

T HE BLEND of semi-settled life and adaptation to differing areas fostered many regional variants of Archaic life. Around 4000 B.C., the "Old Copper" peoples of northern Wisconsin—North America's first metalworkers—began making spearpoints and tools of the copper nuggets that abounded in the Lake Superior area. In New York State finds of the same period are marked by specialized woodworking tools—adzes and gouges—along with slate knives and points. In all the regional variety of the Archaic Period, however, one site remains the most unusual and intriguing of all.

The Poverty Point earthworks in northeastern Louisiana would be impressive for *any* era of North America's prehistory. Before erosion destroyed some of them, six concentric ridges, interrupted by radial alleyways, shaped an octagon three-quarters of a mile across. On its outer edge rises a huge irregular mound; two others—perhaps bird effigies—lie in the vicinity. Radiocarbon readings date them around 1000 B.C., perhaps slightly earlier.

Deep refuse deposits excavated between the ridges resemble those of a large town, and the archeologists who investigated Poverty Point estimate that some 600 houses stood there. At least 33 satellite sites, scattered up and down the Mississippi Valley for several hundred miles, duplicate many of the unusual artifacts of the main site.

Among these are the "Poverty Point objects"—small baked-clay

*Trumpeting in rage and pain, a mammoth struggles in treacherous marsh-
land as his attackers close in. Their Clovis points, lashed with sinew to
stout wooden shafts, far surpassed earlier weapons; one archeologist has
called the grooved stone speartip the "atomic bomb" of its era. Within a
thousand years after their first appearance about 10,000 B.C., such
projectile points had spread throughout much of North America.*

balls, cylinders, or bicones, often decorated by grooving, punching, or squeezing—that number in the tens of thousands. The Indians heated them for use in pit baking or for bringing water to a boil.

"Most of the clay balls in a given pit," noted archeologist Clarence H. Webb, "are of a single type, indicating the individual housewife's preference for a certain shape or decoration."

Poverty Point stoneworkers excelled in their craft. They ground and polished hematite and other hard stone into plummets, atlatl weights, or other small artifacts and ornaments. Flint, chert, or quartzite they chipped into blades, points, and thousands of tiny delicate perforators and cutting tools. True to its period is the extreme rarity of clay pottery at Poverty Point, but there are crude solid-clay figurines, always female, and sometimes pregnant—possibly fertility symbols. Most interesting are the earthworks themselves, for they anticipate others that would not appear for many centuries, and then far to the north. Until more excavation is carried out, Poverty Point—its nature, its economy, and its relationships to other sites—must remain a puzzle.

At the same time the Archaic peoples of the eastern United States were gaining a livelihood by hunting, gathering, and fishing, others some three thousand miles to the south were following similar pursuits. Around 2000 B.C. a village, now known as Huaca Prieta, lay quietly on the Pacific coast of what would someday be northern Peru.

The several hundred people of Huaca Prieta lived by net fishing and by cultivating small plots of squash and lima beans. Gourds substituted for pottery, not yet known to them. They dug their dwellings—of one or two rooms—into their own huge refuse mound and roofed them with whale bones or wooden beams.

Huaca Prieta was most remarkable for its art. The preservation of fragments of cotton cloth, basketry, and incised gourds gives a rare glimpse of the leisure occupations and artistic abilities of these ancient Peruvians and their neighbors. By microscopic examination of the textile fragments archeologist Junius B. Bird, excavator of Huaca Prieta, reconstructed figures of men, sea creatures, and animals woven into the cloth in differing textures, or by the use of colored yarns. These and the incised gourds reflect a beginning of Peruvian art. When corn was introduced to the neighboring highlands around this time, the stage was set for the full flowering of culture in western South America.

A LTHOUGH environment never fully determines man's way of life, it does limit his cultural alternatives. The ancient populations of the central and eastern United States, interior Mexico, and western South America responded to a game-rich environment by becoming hunters. Other peoples in the earliest periods of American prehistory reacted in their own way to differing surroundings. Survival in the Arctic, for example, was just such an adjustment. So was life at Danger Cave, a site within Utah's Great Basin, the driest and—with the possible exception of the Far North—most inhospitable landscape that North America offered its early inhabitants.

The Great Basin arcs from southern Nevada through Utah and ends at the Rockies. No streams drain out of this vast desert, and there is no evidence that the climate has undergone any real change in the past 10,000 years. Thus the harsh land offered hardly more to the ancient

Seed of New World civilizations, corn grew as a wild grass in Middle America before 5000 B.C. The tiny cob at top and the loose-husked ear, both from San Marcos Cave in south-central Mexico, date from before 4000 B.C. Farmers crossed the strains they found to produce, by about 1000 B.C., a small hybrid, bottom. (All drawn about half actual size.)

RICHARD SCHLECHT, AFTER PAUL C. MANGELSDORF, ET AL., "PREHISTORIC WILD AND CULTIVATED MAIZE," IN DOUGLAS S. BYERS, ED., "THE PREHISTORY OF THE TEHUACAN VALLEY," VOL. 1, UNIVERSITY OF TEXAS PRESS, 1967

inhabitants of Danger Cave than it did to the Paiute and other "Digger Indians" who lived in the Great Basin during the 19th century.

Man lived in Danger Cave and nearby rock-shelters as early as the ninth millennium B.C., at the same time Folsom hunters camped at Lindenmeier some 600 miles east, across the mountains. The Danger Cave people were not true nomads, but seasonal wanderers, and they and their descendants exemplify the successful use of limited natural resources—a pattern of life that archeologists call Desert Culture.

The twin hallmarks of Desert Culture, whether they appear in the Great Basin itself or in similar contemporary cultures of southern Mexico, are the shallow milling stone and basketry.

Twined reed fragments from Danger Cave are among the oldest examples of basketry known, and the talent involved in the craft extended to the making of traps, nets, and snares to capture such small animals as porcupines, rats, mice, and gophers. On the milling stones the cave dwellers ground parched wild plant seeds, which they probably made into gruels to supplement a diet of hairy roasted meat.

The importance of the widespread Desert Culture far outweighs its superficial plainness, for its way of life—based as it was on the gathering of wild grasses and other plant foods—more than any other lifestyle that developed in ancient America set the stage for the earliest-known steps toward agriculture.

If any single thing shaped destinies in the New World before the Europeans came, it was corn. The plant fostered and sustained the civilization of Middle America and—along with the potato—that of the Peruvian highlands. It provided the basis of life for those who raised the large temple mounds in the southeastern United States and for the peoples who erected the imposing cliff dwellings and irrigation systems of the Southwest. Thus it is no coincidence that the Quetzalcóatl myth of Middle America refers to that great hero-god as the bringer of civilization in the guise of corn.

The honor of the discovery of the New World's earliest cultivated corn belongs largely to one man—Richard S. MacNeish of the Robert S. Peabody Foundation for Archaeology in Andover, Massachusetts. During the late 1950's he searched long and hard across Middle America. In dry caves in northeastern Mexico and in rock-shelters in Chiapas State in the extreme southeast, he found cobs of an early hybrid corn. But none was primitive enough. Finally, in 1960, MacNeish narrowed his hunt to the highlands of south central Mexico.

"Oaxaca yielded nothing of interest," he later wrote, "so I moved on to Puebla to explore a dry highland valley known as Tehuacán. My local guides and I scrambled in and out of 38 caves and finally struck pay dirt in the 39th."

It was Coxcatlán Cave, and in the lowest of 28 successive occupation zones the archeologist and his assistants found three tiny primitive cobs. Their age: about 5,600 years—500 years older than any domesticated corn then known. A walking survey of the whole valley, from its cactus-and-scrub-covered floor to the oak-fringed hilltops, revealed 454 archeological sites ranging from simple shelters to cities. MacNeish selected a dozen for intensive excavation and, during four seasons of digging, the full story of man's transition from hunting and gathering to full-fledged agriculture came to light.

People had lived in the Tehuacán Valley from about 10,000 B.C. onward. Until 7000 B.C., like most of their counterparts in the Americas, they were hunters and gatherers. After that they began to plant squash, avocados, and beans, but most of their food still came from the collecting of wild grasses, among them corn.

No one knows how the first corn came to be planted, but more than likely the process of its cultivation was long and slow—a fortuitous combination of accident and experiment that perhaps saw tiny sprouts coming up on the debris piles around the campsites. By 5000 B.C. domesticated corn and other plants, as evidenced by findings in cave strata, accounted for 10 percent of the Tehuacán diet, and by 3400 B.C. the figure had risen to 30 percent.

Seventeen hundred years later Middle America was a farmer's world. Small rustic settlements dotted the landscape wherever crops would grow—along the shores of the great lake now covered by Mexico City, in the Valley of Oaxaca to the southeast, and in the hot lowlands along the Gulf of Mexico and in coastal Guatemala. The inhabitants cultivated corn, beans, and squash, the three staples that still form the basic diet of the land. They ground corn on concave stones called *metates* with smaller handstones, or *manos*—both still frequently found among house sites—and supplemented their diet with small game and fish. Dwellings were simple affairs, generally rectangular and thatched, with walls of mud brick or mud-plastered poles. Pottery, known since 2300 B.C. in the Tehuacán Valley, had become a minor art form in the ensuing centuries, with varying styles of shape, painting, and decoration.

Perhaps the most characteristic products of these villages are the solid-clay figurines that archeologists have found in great numbers at living sites and in refuse piles. These tiny human effigies are always female, and nearly always naked. Some wear loincloths or small skirts, others turbanlike headdresses. Facial features were merely punched into the wet clay, sometimes into podlike appliqués that served as eyes and mouth. From the number and character of these figurines, it is hard for archeologists to interpret them as anything but household fetishes connected with fertility, an idea natural to a farming people. If so, they herald the rise of religion in Middle America, but religion without well-defined gods. These, as archeologist Ignacio Bernal put it, "were not yet born."

AGRICULTURE, slow as it was to develop and diffuse from Middle America to other centers, held the key to greatness. Settled agricultural life reached the Peruvian highlands about 2000 B.C., and came to the southwestern and southeastern United States around the time of Christ.

The story from then on would "be no longer a struggle of man against the forest but a struggle of man against man," wrote archeologist Joseph R. Caldwell of the University of Georgia. "It will be the story of peoples who now have some economic surplus, of expanding populations and the seizure of territory. It will be a tale of some who now have time to strive for beauty in many of the things they make, of people who can afford to devote material wealth to achieve efficiency in the world of the spirit, and to secure the status and comfort of their dead in the world of the hereafter."

Plastic sheet unfurls across a dig at Murray Springs, Arizona, a protection against an approaching thunderstorm. Cloudbursts interrupt the investigation of this mammoth-kill site —and threaten its destruction by erosion.

SAM ABELL

44

Bull elk shepherds cows and calves in snowy Yellowstone National
Park. Trailing such migratory game, Stone Age hunters inched
eastward out of Asia, eventually crossing the Bering land
bridge into the Americas at least 12,000 years ago.

WILLIAM ALBERT ALLARD

LIGHTS BLAZE WHERE ANCIENT FIRES FLICKERED

Archeologists' tents glow at Hell Gap, Wyoming, where Indians lived and worked as early as 9000 B.C. The wooded hillside (left) gave hunters a vantage point for scouting bison on the plain below; flinty rocks provided material for sharp, durable speartips, knives, and scrapers. Flooding waters of a nearby stream periodically spread silt over old camps and formed floors for new ones. Tags (right) label the cultures and mark the levels of the artifacts. A circle of charcoal-filled depressions in the Midland stratum marked the postholes of the New World's earliest known house; carbon dating revealed it had stood about 8500 B.C.

Upper Frederi
Lower Frederick
Eden-Scottsbluff
Alberta
Hell Gap
Agate Basin
Midland
Folsom
Clovis

49

IN THE FIELD AND IN THE LAB, ARCHEOLOGISTS INVESTIGATE THE WAYS OF EARLY MAN

Excavating at the Koster site in Illinois, workers peel back layers of prehistory revealing a succession of ancient communities dating back at least to 6000 B.C. Each time man abandoned his settlement here, sterile earth washed down from nearby sheltering bluffs and covered the remains of human occupation on the level below. The soil, meticulously screened for evidence of early man, preserved a wealth of items including bone

knives, flint drills, projectile points, skeletons, shells — and even fish scales. Analysis of the unearthed objects, numbering in the thousands, takes place at various laboratories in Kampsville, Illinois, nine miles from the Koster site. There, in a research lab, archeologist Kenneth B. Farnsworth and Nora Groce, a student intern, examine 1,900-year-old pottery fragments recovered at the Loy site in the lower Illinois River Valley.

UNCOVERING BONES OF BIG-GAME HUNTERS' FEASTS

Three students at Murray Springs carefully clean the fossil skeleton of a mammoth (left); others sift dirt for bits of flint and bone; another removes a plastic sheet that had covered part of the site overnight. Big-game hunters camped here beside their kill about 9000 B.C.; soon after, floodwater deposited a layer of sediment over the area so gently that it sealed camp debris in place. Members of four expeditions sponsored by the National Geographic Society cleared away eight feet of dirt with an earthmover, then began work with trowels and dental picks. Water refreshes diggers (above); a white-footed mouse crouches beside mammoth teeth.

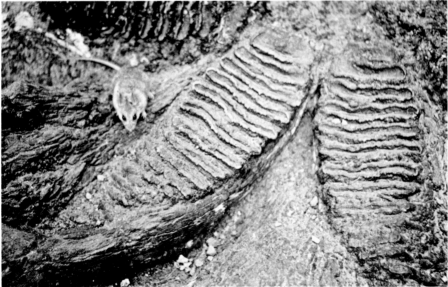

HARVEY STUART RICE

LEAKING LEVEE DROWNS A SITE OF ICE AGE MA

A 10,000-year-old hunting camp lies under the placid waters of the Lower Monumental Reservoir in southeastern Washington, within a protective levee that failed. Investigations at the site started in 1962, when Richard D. Daugherty and Roald Fryxell, both of Washington State University, began excavating a shallow cave in a canyon wall on the ranch of the Roland J. Marmes family. They found tools and bones that showed the cave had sheltered man for some 8,000 years. Fryxell cut a trench from the rock-shelter toward the floodplain below in 1965 to study its geology before

AN ARCHEOLOGICAL TREASURE

a dam, scheduled for completion in three years, flooded the area. At a depth of 12 feet, the bulldozer blade struck bits of a human skull. Fryxell carefully removed them. During the next three years he uncovered other parts of a skull, and elk bone fragments. Radiocarbon tests later dated them about 8000 B.C. These results prompted Senator Warren G. Magnuson to try to save the site; emergency funds in 1968 enabled work to continue, and scientists unearthed bones of two young adults and a child, and several delicate bone needles. In response to public and scientific concern, the U. S.

Army Corps of Engineers constructed a levee to protect the site. In February 1969 water backing up behind the completed dam to fill the reservoir began seeping under the levee faster than pumps could remove it. Toiling around the clock, work crews spread plastic sheeting over the area. Dump trucks then buried the results of seven years of labor under tons of sand. Archeologists hope someday to uncover the site again; meanwhile, Fryxell continues his studies of the geology of the region. At left he compares a sample of volcanic ash with a standard color chart for his notes.

ALASKAN SITES DISCLOSE EVIDENCE OF ASIAN ORIGINS

Crumpled hills and snow-capped mountains of Kodiak Island, Alaska, loom above the fishing village of Old Harbor. Eskimos there depend on the sea, as did their Ice Age ancestors, coast dwellers of the Bering land bridge. At Anangula in the Aleutian Islands, student excavators work under a makeshift shelter (above). They examine a point flaked on one side like earlier tools of Siberia, and found in the Americas only at Anangula. The site, occupied about 6500 B.C., has also yielded stone dishes and scrapers. Farther north, above the Arctic Circle, virtually no soil forms. A recent and an ancient point may lie together on the surface, making it nearly impossible to prove one of them the older. Inland at Onion Portage, though, stone knives resembling 12,000-year-old Siberian artifacts lie in distinct strata. Below, Douglas D. Anderson of Brown University and Mrs. J. L. Giddings, Jr., widow of the discoverer of the site, inspect well-defined stratigraphy in a trench there.

SALESIAN MISSIONS, TORINO, ITALY (TOP); WILLIAM S. LAUGHLIN (CENTER); THOMAS D. GOODALL
(BOTTOM); GUY-MARY ROUSSELIERE, O.M.I., EDUCATIONAL DEVELOPMENT CENTER

OPPOSITE ENDS OF THE WORLD SHAPE SIMILAR CULTURES

Journeying from a caribou hunting ground to a river where he will fish, an Eskimo drinks at the edge of a lake. He re-enacts an earlier migration for a documentary film showing the superb adaptation of his ancestors to a harsh region where the ocean remains frozen eight months of the year and temperatures plummet to minus 50° F. At the southern tip of South America, where men also faced a bitter climate, they responded in remarkably similar ways. Clutching bows, fur-clad Ona Indians on Tierra del Fuego in the 1890's peer at the camera. Like the Eskimos, they hunted land and sea mammals for meat and skins and used the bone and ivory for tools. Barbed points of carved whale bone (immediately below) tipped harpoons at Chaluka on Umnak Island in the Aleutians a thousand years ago, and also at Tierra del Fuego (bottom).

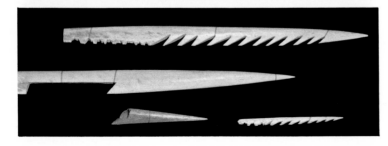

58

3

MIDDLE AMERICA

*Corn farmers under the sway of a profusion of gods
achieve enduring splendor in the jungles and highlands of Middle America*

TO THE CONQUISTADOR Hernán Cortés, who knew it well, the face of
Mexico resembled crumpled parchment. To the six of us, traveling it
450 years later, the country showed varied landscapes, ranging from
ice-capped volcanoes glistening in a hazeless dawn near Mexico City
to the flat forested desolation of the far coast of the Yucatán Peninsula
some 800 miles eastward, where deserted Maya temples still stare out
over the blue-green waters of the Caribbean Sea.

At our home in Springfield, Virginia, we had prepared for our trip
to Middle America by spending many evenings in our library gathered
around the archeological map of that area which I had compiled for the
National Geographic Society.

"The land makes a big funnel shape—except for the Yucatán Peninsula," Gregg observed.

His comparison was apt. Middle America—the region anthropolo-
gists call Mesoamerica—begins in northern Mexico as a wide desert
plateau fringed by mountain peaks and coastal plain, and ends in the
mountains that reach southward to the Isthmus of Panama. Its total
area is less than five times the size of Texas, yet it embraces nearly all
the extremes of topography and climate to be found anywhere on earth.

Geographers separate Middle America's terrain into two basic divi-
sions: the cool highlands that form the core of central Mexico and
southern Guatemala; and the moister *tierra caliente,* or "hot land," the

*A high civilization reaches full magnificence: Temple I at Tikal, principal
city of the Classic Maya period (A.D. 300-900), rises over a great plaza
in the rain forest of Guatemala. Its origins may trace to a shadowy ancient people known as the Olmecs, makers of the 6-foot-high head above.*

GORDON W. GAHAN (OPPOSITE) AND JOHN F. DORR, N.G.S. STAFF

fringing lowlands that shape most of the long shoreline. Both played a key role in the story of Middle American civilization.

That story began in the second millennium B.C. when corn farmers forged a pattern of culture that would continue for nearly 3,000 years. Archeologists usually divide this long span into three major time periods that roughly reflect the progress of peoples and places: Preclassic, from 2000 B.C. to about A.D. 300; Classic, between A.D. 300 and 900; and Postclassic, from A.D. 900 to the Spanish Conquest.

The complicated course of Middle American civilization was wrought by many different peoples whose dramas often overlapped on the vast stage of the landscape. They included the little-known Preclassic Olmecs of Mexico's Gulf coast lowlands; the Classic Period dwellers of Teotihuacán, a metropolis that endured for centuries on central Mexico's high plateau; the Zapotecs and Mixtecs in the misty hills of Oaxaca to the south; and — far to the east — the Lowland Maya, whose priestly obsession with astronomy, astrology, and the passage of time imparted uniqueness to civilization on the Yucatán Peninsula. Later, Tula, capital of the Toltecs, would succeed Teotihuacán and set the militaristic pattern of the Postclassic Period; and finally the Aztecs would follow the Toltecs onto the same tableland and create the splendor that greeted the soldiers of Cortés in the autumn of 1519.

To begin our own journey we went first to Mexico City, then headed eastward by train toward Veracruz State. The cars wound slowly out of the deep valleys that gash the edge of the Mexican Plateau, and onto a hot, humid plain of evergreen jungles patched with grassland and laced with wide sluggish rivers. Just before an evening torrent of rain obscured the landscape, three-year-old David saw what looked to him like pyramids to the north, but actually the shapes were the dark peaks of the Tuxtla Mountains along the Gulf of Mexico — a mass of basalt that rises to interrupt the monotony and mark the geographic midpoint of one of the richest archeological zones of Middle America.

We were in southern Veracruz State, land of the Olmecs, who inhabited this coastland in the centuries just before the Spanish arrived. Confusingly enough, however, their name has become — in archeological reports — the label for a still-more-obscure people who preceded them by some 2,700 years.

Sites of high culture mark Middle America, those lands of modern Mexico and Central America where conquering explorers from Spain found civilized men. Even then, Olmec centers lay forgotten; immemorial but empty cities succumbed to encroaching jungle; and Aztec legend told of bygone and insurpassable glory.

I T WAS NEAR THE WESTERN SLOPES of the Tuxtla Mountains, I recalled, that the first remarkable Olmec discovery came to light. In 1858 an Indian laborer clearing jungle growth near Tres Zapotes saw what appeared to be a huge inverted kettle buried in the dark soil. Hurried excavation crushed hopes of hidden treasures — the object was an enormous human head carved of stone, its thick, stolid features and sharply defined helmetlike cap skillfully wrought from coarse dark basalt.

In 1925 archeologist Frans Blom and anthropologist Oliver La Farge pushed into the marshes near the mouth of the Tonalá River, a hundred miles east of Tres Zapotes. There at La Venta, among jungle-covered mounds and tumbled altars, they too found a stone head, even larger than the one at Tres Zapotes. Who had shaped these strange faces, and when? The questions led Matthew W. Stirling into the land of the Olmecs in 1938. Later, National Geographic Society-Smithsonian Institution expeditions revealed the full splendor of the Preclassic

GULF OF MEXICO

CARIBBEAN

SEA

Dzibilchaltún
Mayapán
Chichén Itzá
Uxmal
Tulúm

El Tajín

a

eotihuacán

nochtitlán
Zempoala

Etzná

la

Tres Zapotes

Becán
Xpuhil

lán Cave
LaVenta

San Lorenzo
Palenque
Tikal
Altun Ha

nte Albán
Mitla

Nebaj

Copán
Kaminaljuyú
Monte Alto

PACIFIC

OCEAN

Olmecs. The culture proved so remarkable that even the colossal heads
—12 are now known—seem quite normal in its context.

The Olmecs suddenly appeared on the Middle American scene
around 1200 B.C., when their religious centers—the first that archeologists know of in Middle America—began rising like the cathedral
towns of medieval Europe to hold sway over surrounding areas.

One was San Lorenzo, west of the Coatzacoalcos River, about 40
miles south of the Tuxtla Mountains.

"San Lorenzo is not very big as sites go," Yale University archeologist Michael D. Coe, its principal excavator, once told me, "but it must
be realized that as we now see it the entire plateau with all its ridges
and ravines is an artifact on a gigantic scale."

Not only did the Olmecs build a ceremonial center at San Lorenzo
around 1150 B.C., they also constructed—with baskets of earth—much
of the spur upon which it rests, nearly three-quarters of a mile long,
half a mile wide, and rising 150 feet above the river plain. On it lies a
system of mounds, plazas, and reservoirs. Man-made ridges that jut
from the south end of the site contain, by all indications, the greatest
treasure of Olmec monumental art in existence. Sometime around 900
B.C., in organized destruction, the people defaced and buried in rows
their great sculptures, including six colossal heads uncovered by
erosion. Olmec civilization had come to an end for San Lorenzo.

What moved the Olmecs to such prodigious efforts? Like their ancestors in the land, they were corn farmers who tilled the river bottom-
lands where annual floodings such as those of the Nile in ancient

Egypt periodically renewed the fertility of the soil. Unlike the simpler farmer's world that preceded it, however, that of the Olmecs was dominated by powerful chieftains and a persuasive religion.

Archeological evidence alone can never totally reconstruct any ancient religion. So it is with the religion of the Olmecs, and unfortunately so, for across the gulf of time and culture, theirs seems to me to have had few parallels in the realm of the bizarre.

The central theme of Olmec religion was the were-jaguar, a combination of man and jaguar, typified by beings with flabby infantile human bodies, cleft or otherwise deformed heads, and the drooping, snarling fanged mouth of the feline. Olmec sculptors made its unpleasant form into exquisite figurines of blue-green jadeite, engraved it on ceremonial ax blades, worked it into pottery and small ornaments, and carved it into their monuments of basalt. In so doing they created Middle America's first great art style. From carved scenes of were-jaguars and from the development of identical motifs in later Middle American cultures, archeologists see some of these were-jaguars as deities associated with the sky and rain, and thus ultimately with the earth itself. In all, Olmec religion, with its misshapen gods, its aura of mystery, and the great human labors it demanded, appears as a dynamic yet melancholy exercise that obsessed thousands of people for some eight centuries before their civilization came to a final and inexplicable end at La Venta around 400 B.C.

Jaguar-men, carrying clubs, march across the great bas-relief at Chalcatzingo, Morelos, 200 miles west of the Olmec heartland. A bearded Olmec priest or chief, dressed in jaguar skin and striped tunic, stands brightly painted on the innermost wall of deep Juxtlahuaca Cave in central Guerrero State. In the Valley of Mexico itself Olmec motifs mark the pottery and figurines that accompany the dead of Tlatilco in strata of the first millennium B.C. beneath that suburb of modern Mexico City. Massive carvings in the Olmec style range south through Oaxaca all the way to El Salvador. Smaller, portable works of art have an even wider distribution. One jade pendant—perhaps looted from an Olmec burial in Veracruz—was unearthed in 1973 on Cozumel, an island off the Yucatán Peninsula.

Oldest date of record in the New World: 31 B.C. in bar-and-dot numeration, according to calculations now supported by radiocarbon tests. When archeologist Matthew W. Stirling discovered this stela near Mexico's Gulf coast in 1939 he had evidence that the Olmecs devised the calendar scholars originally credited to the Maya.

WHO WERE THESE PEOPLE? Virtually nothing is known of their origins, appearance, language, or ultimate fate. At Tres Zapotes on January 16, 1939, Matthew Stirling excavated the broken piece of a large monument, its face carved with a jaguarlike mask in a style of Olmec derivation. On its reverse side he found a date in the style of the Classic Period Maya, who used bars and dots for numbers to record a particular day within an intricate calendar system. The date: 31 B.C.—not only more than 300 years prior to the earliest known Maya date, but also the oldest one recorded in the entire New World—suggests that the Preclassic Olmecs might have been Maya who later moved eastward to Yucatán. Michael Coe thinks such a move was possible, and cites an Aztec legend that speaks of a great state in the "distant past, which no one can still reckon." According to the tale, that state preceded the founding of Teotihuacán around the beginning of the Christian Era. Its name, Tamoanchán—not an Aztec word, but Maya—means, by one rendering, Land of the Rainy Sky.

Two hundred miles west and slightly north of Olmec country lies another world. The Mexican Plateau is one of nature's great citadels, so lofty that the lower layers of cloud often lap against its southern and eastern escarpments and transform it into a dark peninsula thrust into a sea of white. The southern margin of this tableland is blistered by volcanoes that march from the Pacific almost to the Gulf coast, where the great cone of Orizaba, highest peak in the land, rises 18,700 feet. Other peaks and ridges of volcanic debris have formed wide flat-floored basins that share the cool climate and moderate rainfall of the heights. The largest of these is the Valley of Mexico; within its northern reaches a smaller valley holds the sprawling remains of Teotihuacán, the first and perhaps the most splendid of several civilized capitals that dominated Middle America or Mexico in the centuries after Christ.

The six of us visited Teotihuacán early one morning by car, skirting the wooded hills that once formed the margin of Lake Texcoco, then crossing the flat plain of the now-dry lake bed. Beyond the village of Acolman, about 25 miles northwest of Mexico City, the road ascends a gentle rise. On the other side lies the ruined city. My daughter Ann saw its pyramids first and, awestruck, pointed them out to the rest of us.

The mood of the ancient city is one of total serenity, dominated by the Pyramids of the Sun and the Moon, whose aura of solid strength perfectly complements the Cerro Gordo and other scrub-covered mountains that bulk above the valley.

Teotihuacán was never a "lost city"—few large ruins ever were, for that matter. Just before the Spaniards came, the Aztecs, knowing nothing of its history, made pilgrimages from their capital across the lake to pay homage at its ruined shrines and were still worshiping there when the Spanish arrived. In Nahuatl, their language, they named the place "Abode of the Gods," and called its principal avenue "Street of the Dead" in the mistaken belief that the mounds that flanked it were the tombs of ancient kings.

Archeologists have excavated many of the featureless low mounds beside the wide avenue, revealing the platforms and stepped pyramids that fronted it. Even their great numbers—no part of the edge of the Street of the Dead is free from ancient construction—do not detract from the airy spaciousness of Teotihuacán. Its architects made skillful use of horizontal planes that, despite the massive sloping walls that rise from ground level to support them, dominate the whole central area of the city.

The Street of the Dead ends in a wide courtyard at the base of the Pyramid of the Moon. We climbed the gigantic structure slowly, for the stone steps are high and the stairway steep. In the rarefied air of the valley's 7,300-foot elevation it is exhausting to maintain strenuous activity, but the climb rewarded our efforts. On the ruined summit, about 150 feet above the courtyard, I balanced against a strong breeze and looked back down the long avenue. The Pyramid of the Sun, higher and larger than the mass of stone under us, loomed to the left, half a mile away; beyond the gentle slope of its front edge, Gregg picked out the great quadrangle of the Citadel, at the farthest visible part of the Street of the Dead, near where we had begun our long walk through the city. Within the Citadel lies one of the most intricate compositions in carved stone in all of Mexico—the Temple of Quetzalcóatl.

Conquistador Hernán Cortés (1485-1547) sailed from Cuba with some 700 adventurers to break the Aztec empire and set up the rule of Spain. Marquess of the Valley of Oaxaca at his death, Cortés had turned the fate of Europe —and of the New World.

That "temple" is actually a pyramid, but it stands in sharp contrast to the severe lines and smooth surfaces that characterize all the others in Teotihuacán. Originally it rose in six steps, each bearing sculptures of fanged serpent heads protruding from feathered collars; these alternate with goggle-eyed beings that may have represented the rain god or the fire serpent, both among the earliest divinities revered in Middle America.

Opposite the Citadel the white rectangle of the Teotihuacán Museum rises in the center of what archeologist René Millon calls the "Great Compound"—a large plaza enclosed by twin platforms so low and ruined that they went unnoticed until surveyors had carefully mapped the site. Millon theorizes that this may have been the marketplace. Whatever it was, the Great Compound and its enclosing platforms comprise the largest structure in area of any at the site.

The eight-square-mile plain that surrounds the city's center holds almost continuous ruins. At the height of its power—around A.D. 500—Teotihuacán had a population of 50,000 to 85,000 people, more than that of contemporary Rome.

Residential areas of Teotihuacán were made up largely of one-story apartment complexes, each covering a city block 230 feet square and presenting to the surrounding streets forbidding windowless walls of plastered stone.

In one complex we wandered through the incredible maze of rooms, discovering for ourselves a part of the everyday life of ancient Teotihuacán. The rooms, though small and crowded together, afforded maximum privacy—and gave access to patios that interrupted the checkerboard of their floor plans. Large rooms, probably temples or chapels, open upon a spacious sunken patio. At one ruined doorway small animal tracks in red paint lead across the threshold, perhaps those of some pet that lived with a child in "the Abode of the Gods."

The bases of many of these walls, long protected by fallen debris, still bear bright frescoes of fanciful animals and angular abstractions in dark red, vermilion, green, blue, and yellow. Many are simple geometric motifs; others show gods and figures that reflect the elegance of Teotihuacán religion. Tepantitla, one of the excavated apartment compounds, allowed us a rare glimpse into the minds of the Teotihuacános. Painted in warm rich colors, the remnants of a fresco there reveal a sort of Teotihuacán heaven—the "Paradise of the Rain God"—filled with frolicking people, animals, birds, and butterflies in a setting of flowers and trees, and in the center the most precious of all imaginables—a mountain of water.

Teotihuacán's valley was no paradise for the farmer. Then as now rainfall was moderate and confined to a few months of the year. The metropolis most certainly sustained itself by irrigation from the San Juan River that winds in a narrow channel through the center of the site, by intensive use of the land, and by cultivation of such dry-weather food plants as the maguey and the prickly pear, which still cover much of the ruined area.

What of the people themselves—the priests, bureaucrats, artisans, and farmers who must have populated such a city? "We have no knowledge of the Teotihuacán language," said Ignacio Bernal, director of Mexico's National Institute of Anthropology and History,

GEORGE E. STUART, N.G.S. STAFF

"and know next to nothing of their physical appearance, since they had the bad habit—bad for us grave-searchers—of burning their dead."

At its height, Teotihuacán was the greatest political and cultural force in Middle America, and its people probably traveled far over the land. The earthen mounds and platforms of Kaminaljuyú on the outskirts of Guatemala City—650 miles away in the Maya highlands—conceal duplicates of Teotihuacán architecture, and its tombs of the first centuries A.D. hold uncounted examples of the cylindrical three-legged pottery common to both sites. At Tikal, the great Maya center in northern Guatemala, the impact of Teotihuacán is reflected in angular bas-reliefs and in the paintings that decorate some of the pottery.

Teotihuacán was destroyed about A.D. 750. No one knows why. Perhaps it had weakened when its population reached a peak and could no longer sustain itself. Whatever the causes, many archeologists blame the final burning of the city on barbaric nomads of the desert frontier to the north whom the later Aztecs would call Chichimec, or "those of the dog lineage." Reported Bernal, who excavated a portion of Teotihuacán, "The traces of the fire are still visible in the carbonized beams which dirtied the whiteness of the stucco and in their fall tore down the splendid painted murals."

South and east of the Valley of Mexico, the land drops into the jumble of mountains that shapes the gentle curve of Mexico's Pacific coast. In the eastern ranges three long and very green valleys come together, and where they meet lies the city of Oaxaca. Before the Spanish Conquest, the Valley of Oaxaca, as the three are collectively called, and its surroundings were dominated by two great peoples who still populate most of Oaxaca State today—the Mixtecs, whose original home lay in the mist-wreathed hills west of the valley, and the Zapotecs, whose ancient gods sleep atop Monte Albán, just outside Oaxaca city.

While in the city we awakened one morning before sunrise and drove its deserted streets in the half-light till the stretches of pastel walls ended at the edge of town. Crossing the Atoyac River, we ascended the steep winding road to the site; the red tile roofs of town disappeared in the morning mist below.

AS RUINS GO in Mexico, Monte Albán seems small, but that morning we found in its mood of great quiet and in the sheer physical beauty of its setting a place not easily shaken from memory. The principal buildings of Monte Albán, some now restored, others still unexcavated, range along the perimeter of the mountaintop, enclosing a grassy plaza with the ruins of other buildings centered in it. As we arrived in the plaza the sun rose behind the ball court and spilled across the cream-colored temples.

The mountaintop was flattened around 600 B.C., archeologists estimate, by its first occupants and was probably used from the beginning as a religious center by people who may have felt closer to their gods there. Little remains of the work of these earliest inhabitants except for a wall of huge irregular blocks partially exposed beneath later buildings at one corner of the plaza. The face of each block bears low relief with human forms in distorted poses of death. The figures are popularly called the "Danzantes," or Dancers, but most archeologists believe they represent the corpses of mutilated sacrificial victims,

Maya head-variant numerals (opposite, counting down first the left column, then the right) represent the numbers 1 through 19, an alternate system to bar-and-dot numeration. Ten is the skull of that numeral's patron, the God of Death; his fleshless lower jaw adds its value to the glyph for 4 to make 14. Glyphs and bar-and-dot numerals ring the ball player on the stone disk above, giving the date 9.7.17.12.14, our A.D. 590. With three symbols—bar for the number five, dot for one, and a shell for zero —the Maya could reckon in millions.

perhaps chieftains from hostile valley towns. David traced a small finger along the lines of the rough stone. He had found the low-relief bird heads, scrolls, and human faces that accompany the Danzantes. These glyphs and bar-and-dot numbers show that the occupants possessed a basic knowledge of writing and of the Middle American calendar.

The sloping, stepped sides and the dominance of horizontal lines in Monte Albán's low masonry pyramids reminded George of Teotihuacán. He had made an astute observation, for it was partially from the influence of that site, some 225 miles distant, that the Zapotecs had blended their own culture, which reached a zenith about A.D. 300 and continued for six centuries. Here they had their ceremonial center; on the mountain slopes below and in the valley lay their scattered farmsteads and fields. Below the plaza surface, and in the fill of their platforms, the Zapotecs built chambers carefully faced with simple geometric relief that framed the tiny entryways, painted their cramped interiors with crowded scenes of ceremonially dressed men and gods, and placed there the dead of their elite, often with large ornate incense burners fashioned in the forms of their many deities.

As we strolled about Monte Albán, vendors began to arrive. One smiling wrinkled old woman draped a black shawl about her and sat regally on top of a temple platform, a box of bottled soft drinks and ice beside her. Several farmers from the valley joined us. They had come to Monte Albán to graze their burros in the plaza and—with luck—supplement their scant income by selling clay copies of ancient gods as well as a few authentic fragments they had found in their fields.

"Would you like to buy some antiquities?" one asked us cautiously, drawing some tiny figurine heads from his pants pocket. "I found these in my cornfield."

"We came only to look, not to buy," I told him apologetically. To discourage looting of the thousands of sites in Mexico that remain unexplored, Mexican law prohibits the export of pre-Hispanic artifacts.

The most spectacular discovery ever made at Monte Albán was not the work of the Danzantes carvers, or of their successors, the relatively peaceful Zapotecs, who suddenly abandoned the place around A.D. 900. Instead it was the high craftsmanship of the Mixtecs, who even later invaded or infiltrated the Valley of Oaxaca and used the earlier tombs of the deserted site for their own royal burials. One of these archeologist Alfonso Caso found in 1932 and labeled "Tomb 7." In the October 1932 NATIONAL GEOGRAPHIC MAGAZINE he reported:

"On the threshold, or vestibule, separating the two chambers of the tomb, and in the center of a great pile of bones, glittered objects of gold—beads, little bells, etc. Strung on the arm bones of one of the skeletons were ten bracelets, six of gold and four of silver. . . . Upon lighting the floor of the tomb, we found it aglow with pearls, golden beads, and innumerable small, flat pieces of turquoise that at one time had composed a rich mosaic. . . ."

In all, Tomb 7 yielded more than 500 pieces of jewelry and objects of art, and with them a wealth of information on Mixtec craftsmanship, metalworking, and religion, much of it paralleled in the few brightly colored folded Mixtec picture books of deerskin that survived the Spanish Conquest. The incredible treasure from Tomb 7 now occupies the place of honor in the Regional Museum of Oaxaca.

Driving through the valley on our last day in Oaxaca, we caught a most unexpected view. The sun had set behind the mountains, and Gregg noticed a series of tiny bumps against the sky on the dark ridge. Other temples and tombs of Monte Albán, now under careful guard, patiently waited to tell their long-forgotten secrets. Next morning we boarded a plane for Guatemala City—our ultimate destination Tikal, in the rain forest of the Yucatán Peninsula.

Classic Maya civilization flowered in the peninsula's southern lowlands beginning in the third century A.D., and Tikal was one of its greatest expressions. Other centers, large and small, crowd the forest from Palenque, 150 miles to the northwest, to Copán, in the mountains of Honduras to the southeast. Tikal's six largest pyramid-temples dominate the ruins. One, Temple IV, is 212 feet high—the tallest standing ancient structure in the New World.

While Olmec civilization ran the course of its last centuries of existence, and a ceremonial center rose on the summit of Monte Albán, man also lived at Tikal, for pottery found on bedrock beneath the later structures dates the first inhabitants at around 600 B.C.

It's hard to imagine a more inhospitable terrain for farmers, who laboriously cleared land for their corn by cutting and burning patches of jungle, but here they stayed. The civilization they wrested from the rain forest between A.D. 300 and 900 stood in brilliant counterpoise to those thriving in central Mexico and Oaxaca.

After our DC-3 landed at Tikal, we went by truck from the airstrip to the heart of the ancient city in the sweltering heat of afternoon. The surface of Tikal's Great Plaza covers some two and a half acres. Structures built upon it and in the adjacent North and Central Acropolises astounded us by their sheer mass. Temples I and II face one another here; the area of grass between them was once plaster-paved. On one side of this open area, beyond rows of carved upright monuments and drum-shaped altars, a wide staircase leads to the platform of the North Acropolis—and 16 more pyramid-temples.

THE PYRAMID of Temple I is so high and steep that neither Gregg, George, nor I, grasping the safety chain as we climbed, dared look behind us. The limestone steps are slippery, even in dry weather, and worn, partly by visitors, partly by the ancient Maya themselves, who probably used the stairway to carry cut stone, plaster, and other materials for the construction of the lofty summit temple.

After several pauses for rest we reached the temple and sought the cool interiors of its three rooms. I pointed out the vault that formed the ceilings. The Maya never possessed the true arch, but instead built opposing wall faces so they inclined toward one another until only a narrow gap remained at the top. This they bridged with horizontal capstones. The use of this "Maya arch" limited the width of individual rooms, and an overambitious architect could literally bring his handiwork down upon himself by attempting to bridge too great a distance or by sloping the vaults too steeply inward.

Gazing from the front doorway of Temple I, we could see the roof comb of Temple II looming directly opposite but slightly lower. These crests with their eroded reliefs crown many of Tikal's major temples. Had we stood in the same doorway in, say, A.D. 800, the scene would

At Palenque, often called most beautiful of all Maya ceremonial centers, Mexican archeologist Alberto Ruz Lhuillier first proved that great pyramid-temples of the New World may hold tombs of rulers—long a matter of dispute. In 1949 he took charge of restoration there, paying special attention to the Temple of the Inscriptions (shown in the cutaway drawing above as complete from 65-foot outside staircase to intact roof comb, a crowning ornamental wall). On examining a stone floor slab containing small holes, he found that it concealed interior stairs. After four fieldwork seasons clearing away rubble packed in by the Maya to block the passage, he reached the crypt where attendants some 1,200 years before had buried a chieftain with sacrifices and sumptuous treasure.

RICHARD SCHLECHT

have appeared very different. The stone of the temples would have borne a coating of stucco, sometimes stained dark red. Carvings on the roof combs may have been painted creamy white or blue and green. Red paint probably covered some monuments and altars as well, their profusion reflecting the Maya obsession with the passage of time. Most of these carved monoliths the Maya erected on the recurring ritual anniversaries of their highly detailed calendar. Others may record the dates of accession to power of the dynastic rulers of Tikal. To the all-powerful priesthood belonged this realm of calendrics and writing.

Most of the population of ancient Tikal lived in thatch houses that clustered between the ceremonial centers. Nearby lay the cornfields.

Honored and then ignored, a Maya ruler left this stela, a stone slab set by an altar but later broken up and used for building at Dzibilchaltún in northern Yucatán. This ruined city may be one of the longest-inhabited of ancient America; for six years the National Geographic Society and Tulane University cosponsored excavations there.

SOMETIME in the last half of the ninth century Classic Maya civilization disintegrated at Tikal and the other centers in the area. The evidence is silent on the causes but not on the effect. Religious activity ceased, stelae toppled, and the temples became common dwellings. People continued to inhabit Tikal, but the old pomp and ceremony of the processions, the dedication of new monuments, and the secret rituals within the lofty temples had ended. Some archeologists attribute the sudden change to crop failure or drought, others to marauding invaders. Perhaps the most likely explanation is simply an overthrow of the priestly hierarchy by the people—the hundreds of stone temples in Tikal only hint at the labor demanded by the overwhelming power of the priests. The question remains open, and its final answer is one of the aims of Maya archeology.

The disintegration of civilization in the Maya lowlands and the abandonment of Monte Albán by the Zapotecs mark the end of the Classic Period in Middle America. Where there had been a long epoch of stability and flowering of architecture and the arts and priestly concern for things of the intellect, there ensued a time of troubles. In central Mexico small states, constantly preying upon and defending themselves against one another, shared the fragmented power of Teotihuacán. Into this weakly organized area again came barbarians from the northern deserts. By the ninth century A.D. they, and remnants of conquered civilized peoples, had coalesced into a great state—the Toltec—that set the warlike ideal of the Postclassic Period. Military power became, under more sanguinary gods, the criterion of accomplishment and remained so until the Spanish Conquest.

The Toltec capital of Tula, northwest of the Valley of Mexico, reached its first zenith during the reign of a bearded priest-king, Ce Acatl Topiltzin, who took the name of the god Quetzalcóatl and led his people through an age so splendid that later Aztecs celebrated it.

"The Tolteca were wise," went a tale translated in the 16th century by the Spanish. "Their works were all good, all perfect, all wonderful, all marvelous; their houses beautiful, tiled in mosaics, smoothed, stuccoed, very marvelous.

"Wherefore was it called a Tolteca house? It was built with consummate care, majestically designed; it was the place of worship of their priest, whose name was Quetzalcoatl; it was quite marvelous. It consisted of four [abodes]. One was facing east; this was the house of gold. For this reason was it called house of gold: that which served as the stucco was gold plate applied, joined to it. One was facing west, toward the setting sun; this was the house of green stone, the house of fine turquoise. . . . what served as the stucco within the house was an inlay of green stones, of fine turquoise. One was facing south . . . the house of shells or of silver. That which served as the stucco, the interior of the walls, seemed as if made of these shells inlaid. One was facing north . . . red because red shells were inlaid in the interior walls, or those [stones] which were precious stones, were red."

The narrative continues with a description of a similar temple, its walls adorned with feathers instead of metal, shell, and stone.

Archeologists spent years searching for the Toltec capital. Aztec chronicles simply called it "Tollán," which means something like "Metropolis." For many years, Teotihuacán was thought to be the place, but by long and meticulous correlation of Aztec tales recorded by the conquistadors, historian Wigberto Jiménez Moreno finally determined that the Toltec capital lay in a valley northwest of Mexico City. Subsequent excavations proved him right.

We remember the ruins of Tula as a dry and dusty place, with the main part of the site built on a hill bordered by cliffs on three sides.

Among the structures ranged around Tula's main plaza and small central altar rise two pyramids, an extensive system of colonnades, and a ball court. Of these, the most imposing is the Palace of Tlahuizcalpantecuhtli, or Quetzalcóatl as the Morning Star.

Atop it, four 15-foot warriors of stone gaze toward the Valley of Mexico as if frozen in symbolic stance between their northern desert heritage and their destiny as conquerors of Mexican civilization to the south. These warriors — uniformed in tall feather headdresses, butterfly-shaped breastplates, knotted aprons, and tasseled sandals, and equipped with stone-tipped darts, dart-throwers, and incense bags — originally supported the palace roof. Other square columns bear similar warrior figures in bas-relief.

T HE REIGN of the god Quetzalcóatl and his bearded namesake-priest was not to last. In Tula there ruled powerful priests of the god Tezcatlipoca, "the Mirror That Smokes." Together the two gods were revered as creator deities, but while Quetzalcóatl was a beneficent god who had granted man the gift of corn, and thus a settled life and civilization, Tezcatlipoca was the black god, symbol of the night sky, related to evil, sorcery, and death. Just as the eternal struggle of these two gods — the struggle between good and evil — marked the history of the ancient Mexican universe, so did the conflict between their earthly factions in 10th-century Tula mark the turning point in the history of that city — and indeed in the history of central Mexico.

Quetzalcóatl the priest-king abdicated and departed in A.D. 987, and the Toltecs — under the new gods of Tula — began a military expansion that by the middle of the 12th century embraced all of central Mexico.

Where did Quetzalcóatl go? Legend says he and his followers went eastward to Tlillan Tlapallan, "the Land of the Black and the Red," promising to return in a year bearing his birth name Ce Acatl, or One Reed. Actually the answer may lie near the northern tip of the Yucatán Peninsula, 800 miles east of Tula.

Gene, George, and I lived in Yucatán for almost three years; Gregg was born in Mérida, capital of Yucatán State; so for us returning meant going home again. Mérida, a low, sprawling Spanish-colonial city, centers on a large cathedral and shaded central plaza; out from midtown lie smaller churches and parks amid pastel stucco walls and barred windows of the older residences. The countryside between Mérida and the coast, 25 miles away, stretches perfectly flat with little soil over the limestone bedrock and only enough moisture to support a low, dense scrub forest except where farmers have cleared the land for fields of spiky *henequén*, or sisal.

Here in the northern lowlands, Maya history—like that of the Tikal area far to the south—began early at such centers as Dzibilchaltún, on the plain north of Mérida, and continued through the Classic Period with the rise of the great stone-mosaic facades that characterize Chichén Itzá and Uxmal, Kabah, and other sites in the hills south of Yucatán's modern capital. But Maya civilization, rather than disintegrating as it did at Tikal, lasted here into Postclassic times. Around A.D. 1000, though, new architecture rose at the site of Chichén Itzá, and it was not Maya, but Toltec, duplicating the warrior sculptures, the serpent columns, the long colonnades of far-off Tula.

A two-hour drive east from Mérida one midday in glaring heat brought us to the Maya village of Pisté. A few minutes later the gray rectangle of the summit temple of the Castillo, largest pyramid at Chichén Itzá, appeared above the foliage ahead.

Chichén Itzá is one of those rare archeological sites still bearing its ancient name—at least its *latest* ancient name. In Maya it means "the Mouth of the Well of the Itzá." The "well" is the famed Cenote of Sacrifice, a sinkhole with sheer walls dropping some 80 feet to opaque green water; Itzá is the name the 16th-century Maya chronicles gave to foreigners who came sometime after A.D. 1000. According to Diego de Landa, 16th-century Franciscan Bishop of Yucatán, the central structure, now restored on two of its four sides, was the temple of Kukulcan, the Maya name for Quetzalcóatl.

Shattered harmony takes shape again as the author's drawing projects the lines of a Maya mosaic representing part of a throne. Found in pieces at Dzibilchaltún, it originally belonged to a vast ornamental facade.

Late that night I entered the moonlit Great Plaza that surrounds the Castillo. With me was my friend Feliciano Salazar, who has lived at Chichén Itzá all his life and is now the official custodian of the archeological zone. We entered the playing field of the principal ball court, more than an acre in extent and the largest known in Middle America. On either side the vertical walls rose from a low shelf in smooth whiteness interrupted only by the long shadows of the two stone rings set high on opposite sides of the field.

The Maya called the ball game *pok-ta-pok*, the Aztecs *tlachtli*. It formed an important part of public ceremonial life over all of Middle America from Preclassic times through the Conquest. The game may have originated among peoples of the Veracruz coast, for rubber like that used for the hard game balls is native to that area—indeed, the name Olmec means "People of the Rubber Country." And the site of

73

El Tajín, Classic Period center of Veracruz civilization, boasts no less than seven stone playing courts. The intricately carved U-shaped "yokes," so plentiful in the archeology of Veracruz, were doubtless worn by players in one version of the game. Ball courts vary in size and form, though most playing fields are I-shaped. That at Monte Albán, for example, has sloping sides and no goal rings.

Heavily padded opponents, either individuals or teams, played on the courts, and apparently they tried not so much to get the ball through the ring—a rare and exciting achievement that allowed the lucky athlete to claim the jewelry of the spectators, if he could catch them—as they did to gain points by keeping it in motion, away from the end zones, and off the ground. One 16th-century eyewitness leaves no doubt about the peril to participants who "would rebound on the pit of their stomach or in the hollow, so that they fell to the ground out of breath, and some died instantly of that blow, because of their ambition to reach the ball before anybody else."

As we gazed out over the huge court we shouted in turn, "*¿Quién se murió?*—Who died?" Immediately scores of strong voices, echoes from the high white walls, shouted back the final syllables, "*Yo, y yo, y yo*—I, and I, and I."

At the opposite end of Chichén Itzá's Great Plaza, a low pyramid and its temple walls bulked above the long roofless rows of carved square columns; we walked toward it, past the notch in the forest border that marks the beginning of the path to the Sacred Cenote. A short climb up the steep staircase took us to the top of the Temple of the Warriors where a Chac Mool—a statue of a reclining human with head erect—stared at the night, flanked by columns in the shape of serpents. We sat on the highest step. To our left loomed the great white shape of the Castillo, and before it several low platforms.

Bishop Landa, who visited deserted and overgrown Chichén Itzá in the mid-1500's, described two of these platforms as "stages ... where they say that farces were represented, and comedies for the pleasure of the public."

The temple a few steps behind us provided a glimpse of life in ancient Yucatán as archeologists of the Carnegie Institution of Washington revealed it when they cleared its interior of rubble and fallen stones in the late 1920's and discovered pieces of the murals that once covered the stuccoed walls. One of several scenes salvaged from the small fragments and carefully reconstructed on paper shows a coastal village. Except for shield-bearing warriors in boats, the panorama could almost be that of any small Yucatecan settlement today. Its white huts, thatched in dark yellow, virtually duplicate those that cluster along the dry-laid stone walls bordering the lanes of Pisté. Several of the mural's 15 figures—some clad in the long white *huipil* that Maya women wear today—engage in tasks still carried out daily in Yucatán: a man with burden held by tumpline around the forehead, a woman before a water pot boiling on its fire, and some figures simply seated in serene contemplation. Such was life in the forested outskirts of the ruins below us. But, as we sat on the temple step, the uncleared bush on all sides showed black, and there was no sound.

"I come here often at night, after I close the ruins," said Feliciano. "The silence is beautiful." I could only agree.

Prologue to sacrifice: a prisoner of war, tied by rope to a cylindrical stone, slumps exhausted by ritual combat, too weak to lift his wooden blade edged with feathers. His opponent, an Aztec eagle knight, brandishes a sword-club set with razor-sharp obsidian. Soon Aztec priests will rip the heart from the captive's body to sustain the life of the thirsting Sun God

RICHARD SCHLECHT

The Toltecs abandoned Chichén Itzá around A.D. 1200, and Mayapán, to the west, became the new center of power in northern Yucatán. That walled city of some 12,000, densely packed with thatch dwellings around a small ceremonial center, represented the last surge of Maya civilization. Overcome by drought and civil war, it declined abruptly in the mid-1400's. When the Spaniards arrived less than a century later, northern Yucatán—and what was left of Maya civilization—had fallen into warring chieftainships.

In central Mexico, Tula, also plagued by drought and by renewed invasions of barbarians from the north, had collapsed. Charred building stones and wooden beams tell us it was swept by fire and razed about the same time the Toltecs left Chichén Itzá. The great sculptures were toppled, cast into trenches, and buried.

After the destruction of Tula, the political unity of central Mexico gave way to chaos, from which small city-states emerged on the fringes of Lake Texcoco in the Valley of Mexico. Not until the 15th century would a single group—the Aztecs— dominate Mexico's central highlands.

The Aztecs, from an unknown home, Aztlan, or "the White Land," entered the Valley of Mexico at the beginning of the 13th century, led in their wanderings, tradition says, by a wooden image of their bloodthirsty god Huitzilopochtli. In 1325, after a stay on the heights of Chapultepec, they founded their city at Tenochtitlán on a marshy island in Lake Texcoco where, as a tribal prophecy had foretold, they encountered an eagle perched on a cactus, devouring a snake. Unwelcome and shunned by the civilized lakeside dwellers of the valley, these barbarians served in turn as vassals of the city of Colhuacán and as mercenaries of the powerful Tepanecs of nearby Atzcapotzalco. A century after the founding of their city, the opportunistic Aztecs turned on their allies, conquered them, and began the consolidation of an empire that by 1519 stretched as far as Guatemala, more than 500 miles to the southeast.

B. ANTHONY STEWART, NATIONAL MUSEUM OF ANTHROPOLOGY, MEXICO CITY

Sun Stone of the Aztecs, 12 feet across and more than 20 tons in weight, sums up their fragile universe. Symbols fill the design of the popularly named Calendar Stone. At center the Sun God still reigns over our age, fated in Aztec belief to perish in earthquake; around him are the four previous Suns, or world-eras, each destroyed in its turn.

Aztec culture was a spectacular amalgam of much that had passed before in nearly 3,000 years of Middle American life. With the Aztecs archeology converges with history, for many of the Spaniards wrote down what they saw firsthand in the decades after the Conquest. One —Fray Bernardino de Sahagún—was uncommonly diligent. His monumental account of Aztec life, from the rearing of children to the biographies of the gods, is the most exhaustive treatise on a New World culture that has come down to us from the colonial period. Sahagún's intimate view of the Aztecs has given them fame that belies the relatively short period of their dominion over ancient Mexico. Since the roots of Aztec culture reach so far back into the millenniums of Middle American history, Aztec customs provide archeologists with many insights in interpreting the remains of the earlier civilizations.

The life of the Aztecs—man and nation—was completely dominated by religion. More, perhaps, than any other ancient people of Middle America, the Aztecs saw themselves as insignificant beings at the mercy of a capricious universe. Their religion seems to us unbelievably complex. Personal and national gods were profuse and each had more than one identity and function in the supernatural hierarchy.

Wars were, in the main, ritual wars. In addition to subjugating peoples and thus providing tribute, they furnished thousands of sacrificial victims whose beating hearts were torn from their bodies on the altars of Tenochtitlán, for only *chalchihuatl,* the blood of man, was worthy food for the sun; the eating of human flesh that often followed the sacrifice was more communion than cannibalism.

THE CALENDAR wove astrology and astronomy into this fabric of religion and ritual. The act of being born placed the individual at once in a niche—lucky or unlucky—in time. Though Aztec beliefs never extended to the extreme obsession with time that marked earlier Maya culture, the systems were similar. Special rites marked the Aztec months, and the New Fire Ceremony—a ritual spectacle that demanded human sacrifice and the kindling of a flame in the ripped-open body of the victim—celebrated the grand cycle of 52 years that symbolized the death of one life and, the Aztecs hoped, nature's grant of another.

Aztecs celebrated their last New Fire Ceremony in 1507. Afterward, the omens began. Sahagún recorded the Aztec legends: "... an omen first appeared in the heavens like a flame, a tongue of fire, as if it were showering the light of the dawn. It appeared as if it were piercing the heavens. . . ." He wrote also of a strange bird later caught on Lake Texcoco: "There was what was like a mirror upon its head—round, disc-like, and as if pierced. From it appeared the heavens . . . the stars. And Moctezuma took it as a most evil omen when he saw the stars. . . . And when he gazed a second time at the bird's head, beyond, he beheld what appeared to be like a number of people, coming massed, coming as conquerors, coming in war panoply. Deer bore them upon their backs. And then he summoned the astrologers and the wise men, and said to them: 'Do you not know what I have seen there, like a number of people coming massed?' And when they were about to answer, that which they looked at vanished. They could say nothing."

Other signs came in the last years before 1519: a temple destroyed by sudden fire, another by lightning with thunder, a comet, unexplained waves on the lake, a woman's voice moaning, "My beloved sons, whither shall I take you?" In the light of the underlying pessimism of the Aztec mentality, embodied in the tragic and meditative figure of the Emperor Montezuma II, the last of these omens tipped the scales of impending doom. A year One Reed (the same designation recurred every 52 years), the predicted year name of Quetzalcóatl's return, dawned in 1519. There came rumors from the east of four-legged monsters with human bodies growing from their backs, of invincible strangers with deadly weapons who came from great houses on the sea, and of a strong, bearded leader. Was this Quetzalcóatl returning as he promised? Montezuma, pondering the omens and the strange new events, hesitated until it was too late.

Alert for any slip of loose rock, author Stuart carries his son David above the restored portion of staircase on the temple-pyramid of Etzná, a Maya site in Campeche State; his daughter Ann clambers before them.

GORDON W. GAHAN

76

THE LONG ASCENT: PATTERN OF MAYA ACCOMPLISHMENT—AND DECLINE

Low sun and imminent storm bring Etzná the brilliance of color that the Maya loved and used whenever possible—in clothing and jewelry and feather ornaments, in mural paintings, on building facades. Mosaic covered the second level of the temple-pyramid (below, slightly distorted by a wide-angle lens). The pyramid contains four zones, unusual in that each has its own architectural treatment. The shrine proper adds a fifth: a five-story building, in effect. For all their grandeur, such structures developed out of houses known from the earliest Maya sites, some 3,000 years old, and in villages today—a hut of poles lashed into walls and daubed with mud, thatched with grass or leaves, and raised on a low earthen platform to keep the floor dry in the summer rains. Preclassic mounds, from before the Christian Era, show stages in this process. Later, these modest homes surrounded great religious centers, scattered in clusters through the dense bush where men burned clearings for their plots of corn. Hoping for good crops, the Maya paid honor to the

four Chacs, or rain gods, each with a color of his own and a home at one corner of the world. The clay vessel at left held incense burned for the Chacs at Mayapán, in the last decadent period of Maya civilization; Maya farmers of Yucatán remember the Chacs to this day. But something in the spirit of Maya life had faltered long before. Priests or rulers ceased to erect stelae bearing dates; the last known date at Etzná is A.D. 810. At many sites in the Maya heartland people abandoned their cities, for reasons still unknown.

**TEOTIHUACÁN: HOME OF THE GODS FOR CENTURIES
AND A RUIN FOR CENTURIES MORE**

Pyramid of the Moon, more than 135 feet high, dominates the Street of the Dead, a name given by marveling Aztecs to the 1½-mile-long avenue through

a ruined metropolis that seemed the work of giants or gods. Its people's name and origin remain a riddle. By the third Christian century Teotihuacán ruled the central Mexican highlands and spread its influence far. But it stood unfortified near the northern frontier of civilization; invaders sacked and burned it about A.D. 750.

THE OLMECS: GREATNESS BEG

Cryptic drama pervades the works of
mecs, creators—more than 2,500 yea
—of Middle America's first great ar
The unique group at left, just as foun
Venta, enacts a mystery. Facing 15 t
ures of jade or serpentine, one of
stone seems marked for sacrifice.
Matthew Stirling, a pioneer of Olmec s
kneels by a colossal head at San Lor
1946. A ritual ax (above) exalts the
Olmec deity: part snarling jaguar, part

MONTE ALBÁN: CAPITAL OF THE ZAPOTECS, CROWN OF THE VALLEY OF OAXACA

At earliest light, the author leads George and Gregg across the Great Plaza of Monte Albán. Here men without metal tools, wheeled vehicles, or beasts of burden leveled a mountaintop to build a ceremonial center. At left, David follows his father past the famous "Danzantes"; these so-called Dancers date from the earliest period of the site, between 1000 and 300 B.C. Their nudity implies humiliation; probably they represent defeated chieftains. Later builders set other Danzante stones into new walls as if at random. From a tomb dating between 300 and 100 B.C. came the mask at far

left, 31 pieces of jade and shell fitted to the image of a vampire bat. Technique and subject suggest contact with the Maya, who associated this blood-drinking creature with sacrifice. Experts confidently ascribe the city in its prime — which endured until about A.D. 900 — to the Zapotecs, residents in the valley to the present, famed down the centuries for keeping stubbornly to their own ways and language. Zapotec architects carefully aligned the buildings of the Great Plaza at right angles, oriented north-south or east-west, with one exception — the structure above, possibly an observatory.

CLOUD PEOPLE OF OAXACA: ZAPOTECS, AND MIXTEC MEN OF WAR

At peace with the world, an Indian plays his flute by the highway through the Valley of Oaxaca. Equally secure among the mountains, the ancient Zapotecs enjoyed life until the troubled centuries after A.D. 900. About that time new rulers entered the valley—leaders of the Mixtecs, a related people from the west, extending their power by shrewd dynastic marriages and securing it within a century. Like their predecessors, the Mixtecs called themselves "Cloud People" in their own tongue, but the style of their arts set them apart beyond mistaking. They proudly recorded their history in brightly painted codices, folding books of deerskin. As goldsmiths they ranked supreme in Mexico. The pendant below displays their mastery of gold and turquoise,

and its symbol for war their taste for militarism. At right, George Stuart and his family explore the stronghold of Yagul, a small town crowded onto a hillside with a fort above. Lower strata here yield Zapotec pottery bits in types known from Monte Albán; higher levels prove Mixtec settlement. The sequence shows most clearly in the ruins at right, the Palace of Six Patios. From the valley towns the Mixtecs journeyed to Monte Albán to bury their kings in sacred ground; its celebrated Tomb 7 has surrendered gold and silver, turquoise, coral, amber, and thousands of pearls. To this day the Zapotecs and the Mixtecs cling to their identities. They united, however, when the dread Aztecs invaded the valley—and managed to save themselves.

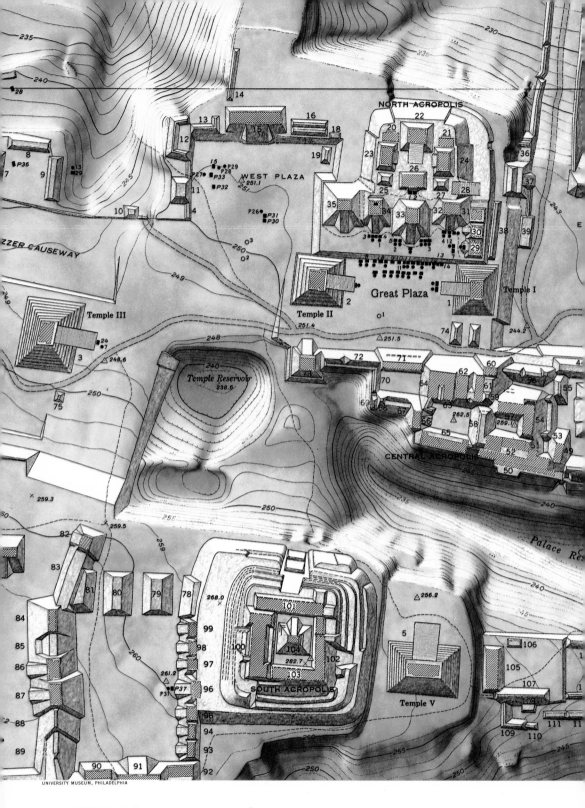

ANCIENT ORDER AND LIVING SCIENCE

Matter-of-fact triumph of modern archeology, this portion of a large-scale map lays bare the ceremonial area of central Tikal, setting for Maya worship during some 1,000 years. Shading and one-meter contour intervals give the shape of the land; relatively high ground probably drew men to settle here, about 600 B.C., for Tikal stood at the edge of a huge seasonal swamp. Drawings render major structures as if intact; hatching slanted down from left to right indicates exposed walls of ruins. All the buildings have reference numbers. In the plazas

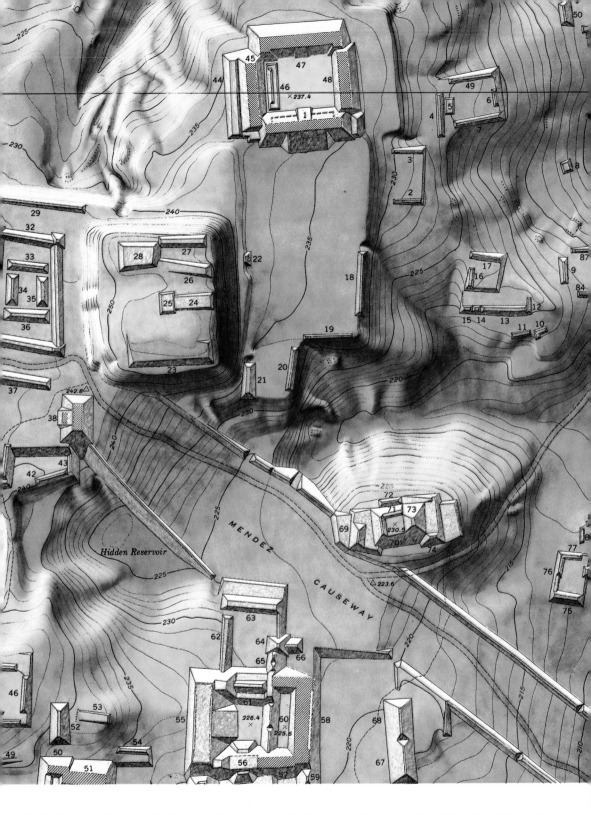

small black rectangles record stelae; disks, altars. Companion maps to this, equally comprehensive, detail minor centers and house mounds extending for miles into the jungle. The series stems from the most thorough study ever made at a Maya site. Skilled teams worked here 13 years, 1956-69, under the auspices of the University Museum of the University of Pennsylvania, amassing many thousands of artifacts, 50,000 photographs, and notes for each. Giving as much attention to workaday remains as to the rich and spectacular, archeologists hope to determine why the city prospered so long—and why, by A.D. 900, it waned.

B. ANTHONY STEWART, NATIONAL MUSEUM OF ANTHROPOLOGY, MEXICO CITY (BELOW), AND GORDON W. GAHAN

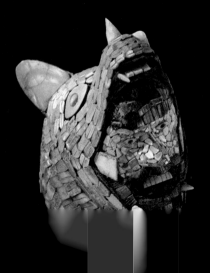

THE POWER OF MEN-AT-ARMS: THE TOLTEC EMPIRE

A pensive Mexican boy at Tula gives scale to Toltec warriors in stone; uniformed with stylized feather headdresses and butterfly breastplates, they gaze blankly ahead as if awaiting orders. Their living counterparts secured a domain in central Mexico about A.D. 900, after nomad bands from the northern deserts blended with the civilizations of Middle America. Building a conquest state, the Toltecs ultimately chose the easily defended site of Tula for a capital and dedicated its principal temple to their god Quetzalcóatl; the "Atlantes" above, and other equally massive columns, held up its roof. The 5-inch-high shell-mosaic work at left, a warrior's head in coyote jaws, helps explain why the Aztecs remembered the Toltecs with awe as master artificers. In Veracruz the Pyramid of the Niches stands at El Tajín, once the focus of central Mexican civilization.

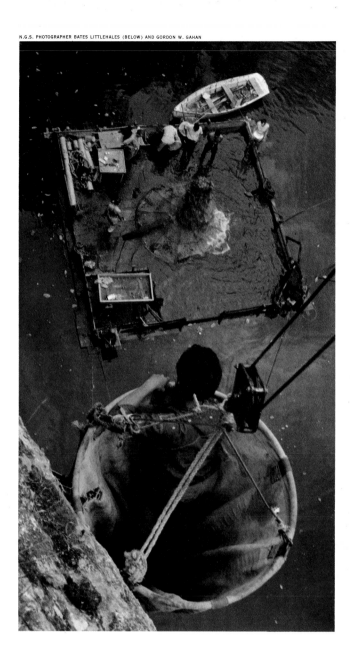

AT THE TIMELESS SHRINE: WATER GIVES UP ITS OFFERINGS TO THE PRESENT

In the limestone country of Yucatán, sinkholes called *cenotes* offer the chief natural source of water during the dry season, and some, at least, seemed holy to the Maya. At the most famous, the Sacred Well of Chichén Itzá, a 300-yard causeway led worshipers from the Great Plaza of the Castillo (left) to hurl their gifts into the depths—lumps of incense, pottery, jade, gold, or a living human sacrifice. Here, in 1960-61, the first archeological exploration with air lift and free-diving equipment recovered figurines, textile fragments, and ornaments of metal. The National Geographic Society, Mexico's National Institute of Anthropology and History, and the Exploration and Water Sports Club of Mexico (CEDAM) together sponsored the project. Above, a canvas bucket lowers a Maya workman to water level some 80 feet below the rim; there the air lift brings relics bubbling up to rest on a wire screen. One rare item: a four-inch effigy in solid rubber.

STRANGE GOD IN A STRANGE LAND: THE FEATHERED SERPENT AT CHICHÉN ITZÁ

Boldly carved, the head of the snake juts from a balustrade at the Temple of the Warriors; beyond, the pyramid Spaniards named Castillo (Castle) gives the god an imposing monument. Ancient among the deities of Middle America, the Feathered Serpent long remained an alien to the Maya. He gained worship and a name (Kukulcan) in their tongue only when victorious Toltecs took Chichén Itzá and transformed its life in their own image. Other divinities came from Tula as well, with the unmistakable sculpture of soldiers and a word meaning "glory." At the shrine of the Temple of the Warriors (opposite), columns embody two monstrous rattlesnakes, their tails thickened to support a now-crumbled wooden lintel, their threatening heads thrust forward. Before them, gazing into the distance, the life-size, sculpted Toltec ceremonial figure known as Chac Mool holds a disk—perhaps to receive a sacrificial offering. This rite became an obsession among their heirs the Aztecs, who feared that without a daily sacrifice the Sun God would halt in his course and night destroy the life of the world. Now at Chichén Itzá darkness brings silence; only bird calls greet the dawn.

MYSTERIES OF TIME: A THEME FOR GODS AND MEN

Visiting Chichén Itzá, the author studies a key to its history: the date A.D. 879, carved in Classic Maya glyphs on the lintel above him. (Salvaged from a later temple wall, it now rests on Toltec pillars.) Though archeologists have found other, abbreviated, dates at the site, only this one appears in the Long Count, a system of specifying a day so fully that scholars can correlate it with our calendar. To the Maya each day was a living god. Their priests, skilled in numbers and in the lore of time, traced the courses of the heavenly bodies. The Caracol at Chichén Itzá—shown at sunset and in the glow of day—evidently served as an observatory; openings in its upper walls give lines of sight that bisect both the setting sun and moon at the spring equinox.

GESTURES SPEAK FOR A SILENCED PAST

Drawn with a sure hand, a seated Maya priest extends his arm in ritual gesture; speech scrolls at his lips echo his voice. Style and technique of this ceremonial bowl reflect the bold freedom of expression that often characterizes the work of the Maya painter. Clay captures the lithe half-crouch of a player in Middle America's ancient game of ball, more rite than sport. Heavy padding absorbed the bruising impact of solid rubber. In northwest Mexico a sandlot version survives. Protected by a leather strap, the player propels the ball toward the goal with his hip only.

UXMAL: A LIVING HERITAGE

Stone by stone, Maya workmen reconstruct the lower courses of the Pyramid of the Magician at Uxmal, carrying on a program of restoration continued by the Government of Mexico since 1938. Their pulley and metal tools are modern, but a scaffold of poles lashed together undoubtedly served the original builders. Here, in southwest Yucatán State, unknown masters brought an elaborate style to its best; its name, Puuc, comes from a nearby range of hills. Making his way to Uxmal in 1840, an adventurous Yankee, John Lloyd Stephens, found "singular but wrecked magnificence." Below, *Casa de las Monjas* (the Nunnery), a misleading Spanish name, gleams beyond a corbeled arch. The Mayas never devised a true arch, but eased the stones of opposing walls closer until a slab could span the gap. Thus even their grandest structures held only dark, narrow rooms.

GORDON W. GAHAN

TULÚM: REMNANT OF A WORLD

Limestone city walls and temple shine surf-white above the cliff at Tulúm, a landmark for mariners today as in 1518, when Spanish ships reconnoitered the eastern coast of the Yucatán Peninsula. Such fortifications appeared in troubled days of foreign invasion and petty local wars. Yet for more than two centuries before the Spaniards confirmed their conquest, the lords of Mayapán controlled a last Maya empire on the peninsula and filled their capital with shoddy copies of the crumbling shrines at Chichén Itzá. Best preserved of these ceremonial centers, Tulúm still contains a wealth of faded mural paintings, Mixtec in style but Maya in content.

GORDON W. GAHAN

MAYA HANDIWORK: TREASURES FOR ETERNITY

Prized above gold in Middle America, jade called into play the highest skills of Maya lapidaries. A spectacular and unprecedented example of their work, the 6-inch-high jade head at right weighs 9¾ pounds; crossed eyes identify it as Kinich Ahau, Our Lord the Sun. A flattened base gave it stability for ritual display. Buried more than 13 centuries ago, it came to light in March 1968 as an expedition from the Royal Ontario Museum dug into a temple at Altun Ha, in British Honduras (Belize); with many other objects—including 150 jade beads from a necklace, bracelets, and anklets—it made up the grave goods of an elderly priest. Probably the miniature heads above, from another offering at Altun Ha, also belonged to priestly regalia. A cache at Nebaj, Guatemala, held the 5½-inch-wide plaque below, unexcelled in design and finish. Pyrite in the same trove, cherished for its golden luster, stained this piece. Such discoveries prove that no gift—however precious the material, however patient the craftsmanship—seemed too dear for the honored dead.

ALTUN HA, CITY OF SURPRISES, OPENS NEW VISTAS ON MAYA LIFE

Stripped of trees and open to visitors coming from Belize City, the Temple of the Masonry Altars stands above the southern plaza of Altun Ha, cleared of six ancient phases of rebuilding over the structure of A.D. 600-650. In that period, while reconstructing the original shrine, mourners left the jade head of the Sun God Kinich Ahau (previous page) with the body of his priest. "The really surprising thing about the head," says its discoverer, David Pendergast, "is finding it here, not at a major center but in a medium-size trading city at the edge of Maya country. Why here? We just don't know. And the temple is unique in several ways: remains of two long rooms on the first landing, for instance. At each stage this temple shows a whole range of architectural experiments not known anywhere else. Within their tradition, the Maya everywhere showed great imagination and flexibility—more than scholars recognized in the past. This, I think, is a clue to the long life of this civilization, and its sense of serenity." At right, Dr. Pendergast holds a long strand of shell beads in warm tones of rose and the restrung jade necklace from the priest's tomb. Jade's color to the Maya matched that of young corn, staple of their society, the food that sustains the life of man.

4

THE SOUTHWEST

Dwellers in a harsh land reach a delicate balance with nature and create a tradition of brilliant craftsmanship that spans a thousand years

MY SON GEORGE and I made the drive to Wetherill Mesa with Dan Scurlock, one of the rangers who oversee Colorado's Mesa Verde National Park and its extraordinary wealth of Indian ruins. Wetherill is but one of some 20 mesas that form the southern part of the great island of land that early Spaniards named Mesa Verde, or Green Table. On Wetherill alone archeologists have surveyed better than 900 prehistoric sites, working to excavate and restore the best for public view. Most of the stone-and-mortar dwellings, or pueblos, lie on the mesa top—small and well-hidden by dense vegetation; many more nestle in the canyon cliffs below. All were built by the Pueblo Indians and their ancestors the Basketmakers—together called the Anasazi—between about A.D. 400 and 1300.

Dan had met us early that morning near park headquarters on Chapin Mesa, site of the most widely known of the pueblos: Cliff Palace, Balcony House, and Spruce Tree House. "If there's the slightest hint of rain, we'll have to turn back," he had warned. "The road to Wetherill is bad anyway. When it's wet it's impossible."

At best it's rather frightening. For the first five miles we followed the narrow scar of the twisting road up and down the slopes of a scrub-covered wilderness—and for a few anxious moments traveled the very edge of Mesa Verde's main ridge. To our right, 2,000 feet down the plunging escarpment and six miles away, the small town of Cortez lay

Centuries-old Pueblo Bonito stands in ruin in Chaco Canyon, New Mexico, one of hundreds of communities that thrived in the American Southwest after nomadic hunters became settled farmers. An Indian artisan of Arizona shaped the stone horned toad above as a palette to hold paint pigments.

serenely in the wide Montezuma Valley; on the left the ground sloped away in grassy folds—the beginnings of the long flat-topped ridges that finger south toward New Mexico. To my relief the dirt lane curved left to follow one of them. The vegetation thickened; half an hour later we parked in the cool shade of a pine grove. Dan led the way down a stony trail worn into the dark-red soil, and suddenly we stood on the edge of a wide canyon.

"Careful here," he cautioned, indicating a safety rope laid over the smooth rock slope. "Until the accessways to the ruins below are opened to the public, this is the only way down."

Grasping the rope, we backed down in turn over the brow of the cliff. Beyond the steep slope a narrow trail slanted downward among stunted trees that clung to the canyon wall. Wooden steps bridging an abrupt drop in the trail took us farther into the canyon. Before us we saw an ancient stone stairway—a series of slabs set into the rock wall. We skirted the steps and approached the cliff dwelling they had helped name: Step House.

The ruin, an arcing cluster of rectangular buildings and circular ceremonial chambers, or kivas, fills a natural alcove in the cliff face. Both Step House and the cliff are of reddish-tan sandstone. In the clear morning air the play of light and shadow over the sharp angles and wall textures contrasts strikingly with the sheer face of the overhanging cliff.

ARCHEOLOGISTS had begun work at Step House in the early 1960's, clearing the dusty debris from its deserted rooms, strengthening walls, and even restoring the log roofs of two pit houses for the eventual instruction of the increasing thousands who come to enjoy the park's outdoor museum.

"We had to undertake the restorations," Douglas Osborne, director of the Wetherill Mesa Archeological Project, had told me earlier. "Open areas of the park had long been deluged with more people than they could possibly handle. As a result, the average visitor was, in a way, being shortchanged since these educational facilities simply were being outgrown. Furthermore, continuous use was destroying the stabilized cliff dwellings."

Ranger Scurlock said it another way: "Those ruins over on Chapin Mesa are literally being vibrated to death by the almost endless tread of visitors." The opening of new ruins will not be the sole result of the Wetherill explorations. The joint National Park Service-National Geographic Society project there brought together not only archeologists but also more than 30 specialists, including soil scientists, botanists, climatologists—even an orthopedist and an orthodontist. Pooling their efforts, they have studied virtually every aspect of ancient man, his life, and his environment at Wetherill Mesa.

We roamed around Step House for an hour. While Dan showed George the old storage chambers in niches high above the ruin, I wandered into the deep shadows behind, and discovered one reason the Anasazi had chosen this place to build—rain-fed springs seeped out of the sandstone. Just off the southern end of the main part of the ruin, near a boulder that bore scooped depressions left by centuries of patient honing of stone axes, stood two circular structures with sunken floors, half restored with new roofs of poles and mud plaster.

MAP BY GEOGRAPHIC ART DIVISION

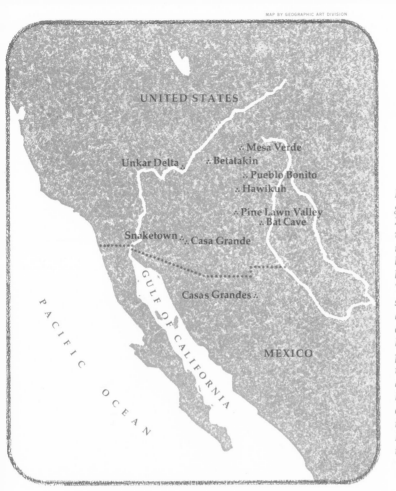

UNITED STATES

∴ Mesa Verde
Unkar Delta∴   ∴ Betatakin
∴ Pueblo Bonito
∴ Hawikuh

∴ Pine Lawn Valley
∴ Bat Cave
Snaketown ∴   ∴ Casa Grande

PACIFIC

GULF OF CALIFORNIA

Casas Grandes ∴

MEXICO

OCEAN

Home to farmers who irrigated their fields more than 2,000 years ago, the Southwest remains almost as arid today as when Indians first began to cultivate corn, beans, and squash there. Through more than a thousand years four principal agricultural peoples developed: the Mogollones, first known to farm and to fire pottery; Anasazi (Basketmakers and their pueblo-dwelling descendants); Hohokam, whose many miles of irrigation ditches made the desert blossom; and Patayans, who borrowed techniques of the others.

"Not kivas, but pit houses," explained Dan when he and George rejoined me, "built before Step House existed."

"Who lived in them?" asked George.

"The earlier Anasazi," Dan replied. "Archeologists call them Basketmakers because most of their oldest remains were found in dry rockshelters that preserved fragments of their basketry and textiles."

Returning to the mesa top, we came to a clearing and looked southeast. Before us, low forest blanketed the ridge of Wetherill Mesa. On the horizon, in northwestern New Mexico, rose the irregular pinnacles of Shiprock. Simultaneously seeing the two places—Wetherill and Shiprock—brought to my mind the diversity of peoples, recent as well as ancient, who shaped the cultures of the present Southwest.

Shiprock is one of many mountains sacred to the Navajo Indians, who call themselves simply *Diné*, "the People." Unlike the Anasazi, the Navajos are relative newcomers to the Southwest; archeologists trace their certain presence no earlier than about A.D. 1500. Since coming from their original homeland in northwestern Canada, they have accomplished much. From the Anasazi they learned crafts and weaving; from 19th-century Europeans they picked up their famed skill as silversmiths. On the other hand their language gives us the word "Anasazi," meaning the "Old Ones." The Navajo story well

111

illustrates the borrowing and adaptation of ideas that must have taken place during the entire prehistory of the Southwest.

More than anything else, the land is one of variety — in its geography and in its archeological treasury. After viewing a cliff dwelling, a visitor might well conclude that it typifies the prehistoric Southwest. We found the opposite to be true. Such dwellings represent only a short chapter in the annals of the Anasazi. We also discovered that the Anasazi were only one of several peoples in the Southwest who took important strides toward civilization between about 500 B.C., when settled village life began in the southern Arizona desert, and A.D. 1540, the year white men appeared in force at the Zuñi towns of western New Mexico.

The story of the Southwest is actually that of the concurrent development of four peoples: the Anasazi, whose plateau lands embraced the great sweep of scenic wonder that reaches from the Grand Canyon eastward through Monument Valley to the Rio Grande; the Mogollones of the arid hill country to the south; the desert-dwelling Hohokam beyond them, in southern Arizona; and the Patayans of western Arizona, whose little-known culture appears to have lagged behind the others in the gradual development of the Southwest. All had their roots in the Desert Culture peoples who had inhabited much of the Southwest since at least 5000 B.C. The slow transition to village life had begun in the centuries after 2500 B.C. — the date of tiny primitive corncobs found in Bat Cave in the Mogollon area of New Mexico — as cultivated plants supplemented wild grasses and small game in the daily diet.

The evidence of the Bat Cave corncobs indicates that the Mogollones were the first of the peoples in the Southwest to cultivate corn, and their pottery dates from at least 300 B.C., the earliest known in that area. Both innovations surely came from the developing centers of Middle America, far to the south. For archeologists, the origin of their pit houses is more perplexing. The only counterparts have a long history in distant Eurasia, with a few occurrences in Alaska's Arctic.

In Chicago's Field Museum of Natural History a diorama re-creates part of a Mogollon village as it might have looked around 200 B.C. Against a backdrop of evergreens, like those that still cover Pine Lawn Valley in southwestern New Mexico, are displayed several low domes of hard-packed mud with dark tunnel-like entryways. One pit house in the scene, scaled to miniature figures, is shown under construction. A shallow circular hole has been excavated and a thick forked post placed upright in its center to receive the radial roof supports.

Mogollones also occupied caves in the area of Pine Lawn Valley, and though excavation of a dry cave — with choking dust hanging in the still air — is one of the more trying tasks of the archeologist, such work in Tularosa and Cordova Caves has revealed much evidence of how the Mogollones made maximum use of nature's frugal yield.

From the forest came wood for implements and for building. Plants provided much of the diet — nuts, seeds, fruits, and berries — as well as reeds for the twined basketry, sandals, and woven mats. The Mogollones fashioned stone into shallow troughlike grinders for seeds and corn, and chipped it into small tools; they collected clays to make the plain red or brown pottery that archeologists recognize as a hallmark of Mogollon culture. Cave remains even show that these Indians filled reeds with wild tobacco and smoked the world's first cigarettes.

Discarded more than eight centuries ago, this carefully woven yucca-fiber sandal remains almost intact. The dry climate of Mesa Verde, Colorado, site of hundreds of cliff dwellings, preserved it. Such finds have shown that footwear styles of the prehistoric Southwest seldom changed — perhaps once in 400 years.

MELVILLE BELL GROSVENOR

The Basketmaker pit houses George and I had seen at Mesa Verde closely resemble those of the Mogollones, and the similarity reflects the general uniformity of southwestern life in the early centuries of the Christian Era. A typical Basketmaker village was Shabik'eshchee, or "Sun Picture Place"—named for a petroglyph on its approach trail. The late Frank H. H. Roberts, Jr., excavated Shabik'eshchee, on the south rim of New Mexico's Chaco Canyon, and found 18 pit houses dating from around the end of the seventh century A.D. The dwellings ranged in a loose arc centered on a large kiva; nearby lay two refuse heaps. The kiva is one of the earliest in the Anasazi area, and excavation of it and other contemporary sites showed further innovations. Pottery—probably an idea from the Mogollones—in part replaced baskets; new inventions included cotton cloth and the bow and arrow. After A.D. 700 many Anasazi built aboveground settlements—pueblos like that at Alkali Ridge, Utah, where strings of connected post-and-adobe rooms formed four semicircles fronting on large plazas, each with a kiva. Other groups continued to live in isolated settlements.

ETWEEN THE 10TH AND 14TH CENTURIES, spectacular clusters of dwellings rose in sere canyons and in sheltered cliffsides—Pueblo Bonito in Chaco Canyon, near the ruins of Shabik'eshchee; Keet Seel and Betatakin in northeastern Arizona; and Mesa Verde. For each of these large architectural showpieces, though, there were thousands of small settlements—like Unkar Delta on the floor of the Grand Canyon, occupied for the most part by no more than three or four families—and these truly characterize Anasazi culture with its successful use of land now considered too arid for farming.

"What has fascinated me," University of Utah archeologist Jesse D. Jennings pointed out, "is that the big southwestern towns did not appear to represent any secular or religious dominance or a central political entity. They were just big towns in a sea of little ones, and apparently represented nothing but concentrations of people."

Life in the large communities demanded great efforts in the harnessing and use of water. At Mesa Verde my family and I had seen only a tiny part of the mute evidence of such works. In a small ravine that drained the mesa top, terraced plots still trapped water and retained precious soil just as they did centuries ago. Dan Scurlock had shown us a reservoir built to catch rainwater on Chapin Mesa, and we all traced part of the channel system through the thick underbrush.

Crops cultivated atop the mesas and in smaller plots in the draws, along with wild delicacies such as piñon nuts and the fruit of the yucca, sustained life in the cliffsides below. I reflected on this life late one afternoon as the six of us stood on a high prominence opposite Cliff Palace, the largest of Mesa Verde's architectural masterpieces, while the red glow of the setting sun filled all but the deepest niches of the huge recess in which it nestles.

Seven hundred years earlier, women clad in yucca-fiber aprons might have lounged and gossiped on the terraces among the close-packed dwellings; others perhaps busied themselves adding final touches to black-and-white ladles, mugs, and bowls wrought and fired from clay gathered earlier. Several men, returning from the mesa-top cornfields or a short hunting trip, carefully descended ladders from the

Stylized figures painted by the Mogollones in black on a white background appear in the interiors of centuries-old bowls first found in the Mimbres Valley of New Mexico. From top: a bird in flight, a pronghorn, a fox, a mud turtle, and a scorpion.

cliff edge, or cast long shadows on the smooth rock face as they picked their way from foot-hole to foot-hole. Others, unseen in the kivas, might have prepared for a secret rainmaking ceremony, a curing ritual, or simply a political meeting concerning some squabble that had arisen in the close quarters of the pueblo.

At the same time, in the rugged pine-fringed mountains to the south, the strong influences of Anasazi culture were transforming that of the Mogollones, diluting it beyond recognition. Between the 8th and 11th centuries, influences and ideas from the rapidly expanding Anasazi took hold, bringing the bow and arrow, cotton cloth, and, finally, aboveground architecture and black-and-white pottery. In Pine Lawn the blend continued until, for some unknown reason, the people themselves vanished from the valley—and from the annals of prehistory—around 1300.

North of Tucson we encountered another of the varied faces of the Southwest—one of dry heat, hot winds, and distant hills darkened by stands of the giant Saguaro cactus. The Gila River, bolstered by a few tributaries in its westward course from the Mogollon Mountains to the Colorado River, relieves this part of the Southwest's only true desert. Such was the setting nearly 2,500 years ago when the Gila and Salt Rivers became lifelines for the Hohokam, another remarkable people of the ancient Southwest.

In the language of their modern Pima descendants *hohokam* means "those that have vanished." Another Pima word, *Skoaquik,* names the principal Hohokam site—"Place of the Snakes," or simply Snaketown.

The site of Snaketown takes up about 300 acres of gently rolling open desert southeast of Phoenix on the Gila River Indian Reservation, home of the Pimas. The story of the town and its people lasted from before Christ until after the 12th century; in its course it saw North America's first successful conquest of the desert by irrigation, as early as 300 B.C.

Cattleman and amateur archeologist John Wetherill sits among ruins at Mesa Verde. He and his four brothers discovered more than 500 cliff dwellings in the canyons south of their ranch in the late 1800's—and gave their name to Wetherill Mesa.

W E MAY NEVER KNOW the full extent of the Hohokam irrigation channels now buried beneath the desert. Estimates run to more than 300 miles, but their extent matters less than the fact that they were built at all, and worked. The Hohokam—undoubtedly by much trial and error—solved problems of silting and gradient by building catch basins and diversion dams.

In small primitive communities a high degree of mutual dependence exists among individuals, particularly in an environment as harsh and demanding as that of the Hohokam and the Pimas. We tend to believe that public works such as huge irrigation systems require a high degree of organization. The Pimas, who around the turn of the century still watered their fields from the Gila River much as the Hohokam did, thought otherwise. They built irrigation networks through simple agreement among a number of men, spreading the labor out during the slack period between fall harvest and spring planting. Such was conceivably the situation in ancient Snaketown. Through 1,200 years of cooperative effort much could be accomplished, and much was. Around the oval clay-walled and brush-roofed pit houses the desert valley grew green every summer with corn, beans, and squash—and Snaketown thrived.

Excavation has revealed little more than the hard-packed floors and

:he cavities where posts stood. Shapes of the dwellings, round or oval, were much like those of houses the Pimas lived in until the 1900's. "We estimated that a hundred houses might have stood in the village at any one time," Emil W. Haury, director of excavations at Snaketown, :old me when I visited his office at the University of Arizona. "We found that the very first houses, though much smaller, were every bit as good as the latest, and not very different from them in style."

Successful conquest of the desert was not the only Hohokam achievement. The sculptors of Snaketown produced striking stone bowls and paint palettes, many decorated with the forms of men and desert creatures; and the potters modeled tiny slit-eyed figurines that remind me of those of the early farmers of Middle America, along with painted vessels in the shapes of humans and animals.

Another achievement, etching, intrigued archeologists for years. Finding shells bearing animal figures in relief had led them to the conclusion that the Hohokam discovered the process centuries before the Europeans did. Final proof came in the form of an unfinished ornament —a white shell with a coating of pitch in the shape of a four-legged animal. An ancient craftsman had applied the design but for some reason had never soaked the shell in a weak acid solution—possibly derived from the fruit of the Saguaro cactus—to eat away the unprotected part and leave the figure in relief beneath the pitch.

Builders of Snaketown and other Hohokam settlements raised small platform mounds, further evidence of their cultural debt to Middle America. A giant basin, partially excavated in 1934, revealed a 100-yard-long ball court somewhat like those of Middle America. Many of the hallmarks of Hohokam high culture began to disappear after the 12th century; the people of Snaketown scattered up and down the river valley; and another sort of architecture began to appear along the Gila.

"... as large as a castle and equal to the largest church in these lands of Sonora," reads the 1694 journal of Father Eusebio Francisco Kino, Spanish missionary to the Southwest and the first European to see Casa Grande, or "Great House."

The huge tan cube of layered, sun-hardened caliche, now weathered and eroded, dominates the flat desert between the Gila River and Coolidge, Arizona, about 30 miles upstream from Snaketown. The children noticed Casa Grande's distant silhouette long before we parked beside the cactus garden that fronts the low adobe museum.

Casa Grande, including the little that remains of the smaller buildings and of the high wall that originally surrounded the entire compound, is now a national monument. The four-story "Great House," still nearly as Father Kino saw it, is sheltered against further erosion by a sturdy canopy of steel. Its main walls, reinforced here and there with concrete, are extraordinarily thick—over four feet near the base— and the structure contains more than a dozen rooms. Its use?

"We don't really know for sure," a ranger told us after we had climbed the short ladder and entered the doorway to one of the cool side chambers. "Household goods were found in the debris inside these rooms, so it may have been an apartment dwelling. Considering its size and height, it very likely served for defense as well."

Distant relatives of the Anasazi built Casa Grande and other settlements along the Gila during the 12th century. Their ruins stand

Checkerboard pattern on this cup remains vivid seven centuries after an Anasazi woman lifted it from the ashes of a wood fire that hardened the clay and fixed the design. Finding several such vessels in a Mesa Verde cliff dwelling, the Wetherills called it Mug House.

WILLIAM BELKNAP, JR.

adjacent to those of the Hohokam, so it appears that the two peoples lived side by side in peace for nearly two centuries.

At Mesa Verde, far to the northeast, the final decades of the 13th century were times of trouble. Timbers cut by the Indians reveal a long series of very thin tree rings—a sure indication of aridity. By carefully counting the Mesa Verde rings archeologists can tell that a widespread drought persisted from 1276 to 1299. The defensive locations selected for the cliff dwellings testify to some strife as well, perhaps among the Anasazi themselves, or with marauders from the north.

By 1400 the Anasazi had abandoned their great communities in the Four Corners area where Utah, Colorado, Arizona, and New Mexico meet and had moved to the south and east, resettling along an arc that stretches from the upper valley of the Rio Grande south to the Zuñi region of west central New Mexico. One group established a cluster of villages within the present-day Hopi reservation in northern Arizona.

O N JULY 7, 1540, Francisco Vásquez de Coronado and his 1,100-man expeditionary force completed an arduous four-and-a-half-month trek from Mexico and stood before the Zuñi pueblo of Hawikuh. Their quest for the fabled Seven Cities of Cibola, based as it was on rumors of splendor generated after the brief visit by Fray Marcos de Niza the year before, ended in bitter, reproachful chagrin; "...when they saw the first village, which was Cibola [Hawikuh]," wrote Coronado's chronicler, Pedro de Castañeda, "such were the curses that some hurled at Friar Marcos that I pray God may protect him from them.... It is a little, unattractive village, looking as if it had been crumpled all up together," he continued contemptuously. "There are mansions in New Spain which make a better appearance at a distance." The harsh and unjust outburst is perhaps forgivable in the light of the disappointment of that moment long ago.

Hawikuh is no more. The lower courses of its great dwelling clusters make a vague checkerboard on a dry hill, and its thick piles of debris encroach nearly to the stumps of the adobe walls of the church the Spanish built there in 1629. After relocation in the wake of the 1680 revolt that temporarily drove the Spaniards from the Southwest, the Zuñis moved to a new town, some 15 miles north of Hawikuh—and there they remain today. Older portions of Zuñi Pueblo can be distinguished by the walls of adobe or plastered irregular stone still visible in the multistory houses. The newer one-story houses are of more carefully cut purple-hued sandstone, and lately the Zuñis tend to build them apart from the main cluster—a modern instance of a long sequence of changes that have marked pueblo history from the times of Shabik'eshchee village. Other patterns are changing too. Seasonal farming camps at some distance from the pueblo have been transformed into permanent satellite communities by the advent of the automobile, the pickup truck—and electricity.

Under the surface, much of the old way persists, for tenacious loyalty to tradition is one of the admirable pueblo traits. Everyone in the pueblo belongs to one of the 15 clans; every male holds membership in one of six kiva societies; and their extravagant ceremonials still punctuate the annual cycle just as in the ancient Anasazi cities. Thus does life continue in the Southwest.

Walls of multistory adobe apartments cover 90 acres at Casas Grandes, Mexico, where cultures of the Southwest and Middle America blended. An underground water system served inhabitants of this urban center, begun about 1050. A labyrinth of terraces and channels laced 11,000 square miles of arid land to irrigate crops. The city crumbled into ruin after invaders—or possibly rioters—vandalized its temples and burned it about 1340. Here a young visitor peers through an eroded window.

W. E. GARRETT, NATIONAL GEOGRAPHIC STAFF

RICHARD SCHLECHT (ABOVE AND LOWER RIGHT) AND KENNETH J. CONANT

RITUALS SUSTAIN PUEBLO-DWELLING FARMERS

Pueblo religious clan conducts a secret ritual in a kiva, an underground ceremonial chamber that also served as workshop and club—for men only. It usually held a circular bench against the wall (below); a stone slab between the ventilation shaft and the fire pit to deflect drafts; and a sipapu, a small hole in the floor for the passage of earth-dwelling spirits. Kivas remain a feature of present-day pueblo architecture. New Mexico's Pueblo Bonito (below left) counted 37 of them and more than 600 other rooms at the height of its development, around the year 1000. Newcomers, arriving after the first settlement began about A.D. 900, lived peacefully with the original inhabitants, eventually taking over community leadership. This later people continuously razed and rebuilt parts of the structure until it spread over three acres (left) and stood four stories high in places. Ladders jut from kivas into a court (above) where women ground corn and cooked over open fires. The Bonitians left about A.D. 1300, possibly driven out by drought or marauders.

CLIFF DWELLERS' DESCENDANTS PRESERVE THE OLD WAYS

Rattles shaking, bells jingling, buffalo dancers perform at the 1924 Intertribal Indian Ceremonial at Gallup, New Mexico, heart of the area settled by Anasazi. Plains Indians possibly introduced such rituals to the pueblo-dwellers. One of 27 pueblo communities still inhabited, five-story Taos, New Mexico, (below) has stood beside Taos Creek more than 500 years. Although its residents elect a governor who holds civil authority, the cacique, or high priest of the old religion, remains powerful. Avoiding contact with outsiders, these people have successfully resisted the influences of Spanish conquerors and missionaries, then Mexican and United States governments. The Navajo ceremonial mask (above) dates from about the mid-18th century.

20TH-CENTURY MACHINES AID THE SEARCH FOR EARLY MAN

Helicopter hovers over rugged Colorado River canyon country. The craft carries scholars to otherwise nearly inaccessible digs and speeds the search for new sites; observers can see the small ruin (above) only when on the same level. With his pilot, Robert Euler (below, kneeling) of the Center for Anthropological Studies at Arizona's Prescott College explores Stanton Cave in Marble Canyon National Monument, north of Grand Canyon. During a probe there, Euler found the animal stick figures in the foreground. An unknown people fashioned each from a single split willow branch, then cached them some 4,000 years ago. Tiny spears pierce two of the effigies, suggesting their use in hunting rituals. Searching for answers to the mystery of the people who made them, Euler led a National Geographic Society-sponsored expedition in 1969.

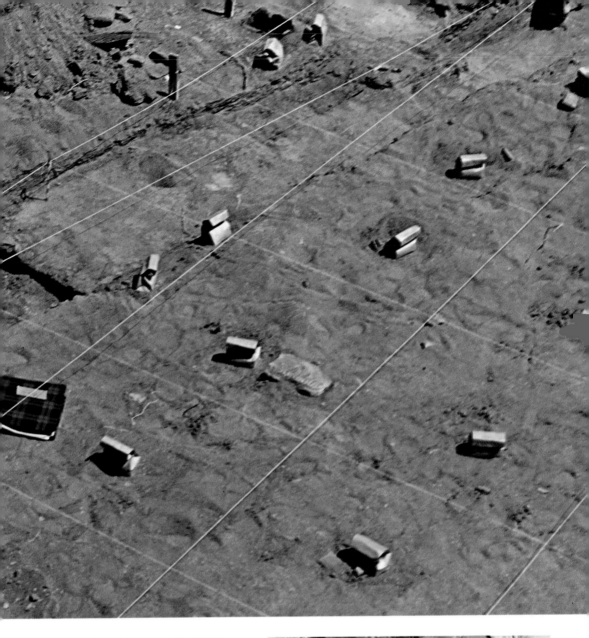

UNKAR DELTA YIELDS ITS SECRETS

Paper bags hold samples of soil from the Unkar Delta site in the Grand Canyon; a grid of twine pinpoints their locations. Analysis of pollen in the soil will enable botanists to determine the area's plant life through the centuries. Uncovering dozens of sites, a 1968 expedition found that three or four Anasazi families moved down from the canyon rim and settled close to the river about A.D. 950. A larger group followed some 100 years later, then inexplicably vanished. Students at left screen dusty soil, seeking even the tiniest clue. Capricious canyon breezes twice blew down the expedition's tents. Temperatures reaching 124° F. made wheelbarrow work an ordeal. Working in burning sun, a student (right) unearths a clay jar.

AT HOME ON THE GRAND CANYON FLOOR

Crisp watermelon slices refresh the crew excavating Anasazi sites at Unkar Delta under the leadership of Douglas W. Schwartz, Director of the School of American Research, Santa Fe, New Mexico (in dark glasses at far right). A helicopter carried the special treat—and all other supplies— to the camp; the men above carefully divide limited rations of beer and soft drinks. The 20 members of the expedition gained valuable experience during a summer of hard work at the isolated spot. Swimming off a raft in the Colorado River (below) gave them some relief from heat and grime.

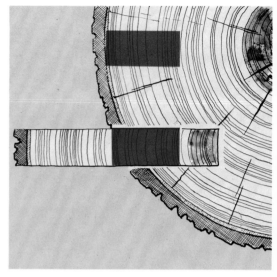

Nature's clearest record of time—growth rings from trees—can answer two questions for archeologists: "When did men live at this site? What sort of weather did they face?" And even more searching questions arise to enrich science as specialists pursue tree-ring studies with today's most sophisticated equipment and methods of analysis.

Above, progress accelerates at the Laboratory of Tree-Ring Research at the University of Arizona, Tucson. William J. Robinson checks an archeological sample of Douglas fir, measuring each ring from inner pith to bark layer with a Henson scanner designed to the laboratory's specifications. He gazes through a fixed optical system, turns a handle to move the specimen and align the edge of a ring with crosshairs, and takes the ring width to the nearest hundredth of a millimeter. At the touch of a button the apparatus records each measurement, printing it on paper tape and also preparing a punched tape for conversion to computer cards. Console lights show all circuits working.

Despite the complexity of such devices, principles of tree-ring research are simple. Usable or "sensitive" trees react to changes in environment by producing rings that vary in width from year to year. In the American Southwest, for example, a Douglas fir or a yellow pine responds to changes in the amount of moisture available, growing thinner rings in dry years, thicker ones in wetter years. Thousands of trees living at the same time repeat this series with amazing similarity.

An expert, comparing sections from such trees, can correlate these matching patterns, a procedure known as cross-dating. Thus, in the drawing above, color singles out a cross-dated sequence showing parallel fluctuations of ring width in two different trees. If you take the smaller sample and count inward from bark to color, you see that this tree lived 26 years after the other one was felled.

Such matching and counting give a relative or "floating" chronology. If you know when the younger tree was cut, you can work out an absolute dating for the life span of both. By this method science has turned riddles of man's past in the Southwest into history.

It began with the sun. Andrew Ellicott Douglass (1867-1962), a versatile astronomer, wanted a method to trace 11-year sun-spot cycles by their effect on weather. In 1901 at Flagstaff, Arizona, he began studying the effects of climate on tree growth, working with samples of known age; in 1911 he recognized familiar ring patterns near Prescott, and saw the possibilities of cross-dating. He pursued his work with vigor.

Meanwhile archeologists began concerted studies of the spectacular prehistoric ruins in the region. Yet their basic question seemed unanswerable: "When did men build these ancient pueblos?"

In 1920 Douglass examined logs from the largest, Pueblo Bonito, and from Aztec Ruin, 53 miles north. He established a relative dating: Construction at Aztec came 40 or 50 years later than at Pueblo Bonito.

Now a classic collaboration began, between teams led by Douglass and by Neil M. Judd, directing the National Geographic Society's archeological research at Pueblo Bonito. The Society sent seven expeditions to

collect wood of differing ages, from ancient sites and from Hopi villages.

As Douglass reported in the December 1929 NATIONAL GEOGRAPHIC MAGAZINE, tact and courtesy won cooperation from Hopi chiefs. Gifts, exchanged for samples from village buildings, included 20 old felt hats—used in making ceremonial masks—and a length of purple chiffon velvet. At times, when the visitors extracted a core specimen from a kiva log, they inserted a bit of turquoise before they plugged the hole—to keep the "spirit of decay" from lodging in the timber.

Year by year Douglass built up a floating sequence of good years and drought, and extended his absolute chronology back from Spanish times. The gap between the two narrowed. He and Judd examined a fire-scarred log at Show Low, Arizona, on June 22, 1929, and knew they were close to an answer: "this charred old stick began its life as a promising upright pine A.D. 1237.... The history within that carbonized bit of beam held us spellbound; its significance found us all but speechless; we tried to joke about it, but failed miserably."

That night Douglass saw that the gap had been bridged. He could prove "Pueblo Bonito had reached its golden age in 1067 and was still occupied in 1127." He wrote: "By translating the story told by tree rings, we have pushed back the horizons of history in the United States for nearly eight centuries before Columbus reached the shores of the New World...."

Soon his "story written in trees" included dates for some forty other major ruins and indicated that men had abandoned the pueblos in times of severe drought.

Studies of ancient weather patterns continue. Above, Robinson plots ring-width values for A.D. 1196 at the Four Corners region where Utah, Colorado, New Mexico, and Arizona meet. Print-out data list latitude and longitude for sites, with statistics on tree-ring growth for each. His pen hovers over Aztec Ruin, source of his specimen, cut in 1240. His findings will apply in a pilot study of man in his environment, including food production and migration, between A.D. 600 and 1500.

"Our gear and methods have changed greatly in the last decade," says Bryant Bannister, director of the laboratory. "In growth-ring terms, progress came by inches for 30 years but now we measure it in feet!

"But the great value of tree-ring work remains the same. Aside from written records, it is the only source of absolute dates for archeology; and bristlecone pines give us a record 7,500 years into the past. Our material provides an absolute check on radiocarbon dating, and has shown important discrepancies in carbon results. So today specialists are rethinking the basic assumptions Willard Libby made in the 1940's when he developed carbon dating—and these involve the whole spectrum of changes on earth through time!

"Tree-ring dates also supply controls for paleomagnetic studies and other new methods that may be valuable for archeologists everywhere. And since trees preserve a millennium-long record of environmental variability, we can better understand the processes of long-range climatic change. Thus tree rings can tell us something of immeasurable value about man's future as well as his past in the Americas."

SANDSTONE DWELLINGS BRIDGE THE CENTURIES

Hands grasp rough ladders and feet cross ancient courtyards, recapturing the feel of 13th-century pueblo life for visitors to Mesa Verde National Park. A ranger (below) points out a kiva at Cliff Palace, cleared of rubble and partially restored. The site appeared in 1896 (left) much as it had when discovered six years before. Early collectors stripped the rooms of artifacts; today, visitors—more than half a million in 1972—explore the reinforced, but still fragile, buildings. Seeking to offer more areas to the public, the National Park Service, aided by grants from the National Geographic Society, in 1958 began to study sites at nearby Wetherill Mesa and in 1973 opened Long House, second largest cliff dwelling in the park.

5

THE SOUTHEAST

*Flourishing cultures gather magnificence from a diversity
of peoples north to the Ohio Valley and west to the Mississippi*

OF ALL THE RIVERS that fall from the lush green hills of north Georgia, our favorite is the Etowah. Near Cartersville it flows gently westward through a wide valley beneath huge overhanging trees, just as it must have some 700 years ago when an energetic people built the big flat-topped Etowah Mounds beside its quiet waters.

Today the river attracts families from nearby farms who gather on summer afternoons to fish from its banks. They, like most of the valley's inhabitants, can tell you something of the mounds, for the Etowah site and the discoveries made there are almost as well known to them as to the archeologists.

To us Etowah has a special meaning. Gene and I first met there during excavations in the summer of 1954, when she was an archeology student with Arthur R. Kelly's field school from the University of Georgia, and I was assisting Lewis H. Larson, Jr., director of a dig sponsored by the Georgia Historical Commission.

The place looked quite different when we took the children to visit 15 years later. Shaded paths had replaced the thick undergrowth along the river; the mound slopes were cleared of brambles; the tall grass in the plaza was neatly mowed.

Three principal mounds—archeologists label them simply A, B, and C—dominated the ancient site. The Etowans had surrounded themselves with a protective moat by digging a channel that carried river

*Platforms for temples and houses—dating between 1200 and 1500—flank a
ceremonial plaza and a museum at Moundville, Alabama, a center for the ritualistic Southern Cult. Diverse southeastern cultures built thousands of such
mounds. Ancient Ohio Hopewell people shaped the mica bird claw (above).*

GORDON W. GAHAN (OPPOSITE) AND OHIO HISTORICAL SOCIETY, COLUMBUS

Archeological Southeast encompasses an ancient cultural region larger than the geographic area of toda This map shows sites of principal ceremonial center: erected by three great south eastern cultures—Adena, Hopewell, and Mississippia —and locates important aboriginal settlements. Indian burial, effigy, and temple mounds, built in the centuries between 1000 B.C. and A.D. 1500, lie scattered from the Mississippi Valley to the Atlantic Ocean.

water in a great semicircle encompassing an area of some 40 acres. With the dirt from the moat they built the mounds.

"Just how *did* they build them?" George asked as we walked across the field toward the largest, Mound A.

"Basketload by basketload," explained Gene. "In fact, trenches through mounds like these often reveal cross-sections of the small domes of earth where individual loads were dumped. The builders' painfully slow labors eventually created what must have been one of the most impressive communities of its time."

Mound A rises steeply from the plaza to a height of more than 60 feet. Single file, we made the long hot climb up the front ramp, now restored with steps of railroad ties. On top, more than half an acre of flat ground invited a peaceful stroll and gave us an awesome view of the valley fields and distant mountains.

Since 1953, when the Georgia Historical Commission acquired the site, the story of Etowah has been one of meticulous excavation that has shed much light on the flourishing settlement and the mixture of religion and politics that governed it. Posthole patterns in the many layers of cultural debris indicate that Etowah, at its peak, was crowded with square thatched houses, some occupying places of prominence atop the mounds. Excavation of Mound C showed that the Etowans used it principally as a burial mound for the elite. Those interred during one of several construction stages of the mound reflect in their rich tomb offerings, as one archeologist put it, "as complicated a series of mortuary rituals as could be conceived."

To understand better the Etowans' way of life—and death—in the centuries around A.D. 1400, one must first view the greater area of the eastern United States and the diverse cultures of the preceding 2,400 years. Mounds play a large part in the known story.

More than 25 years of painstaking excavation have revealed that, contrary to early belief, no single race of "mound builders" was responsible for the vast array of earthworks that pioneer settlers in the East chanced upon—and wondered about.

Sometime before 1781 a distinguished Virginian found his scientific curiosity piqued by a low mound beside the Rivanna River near Charlottesville, and he "determined to open and examine it thoroughly." In so doing, Thomas Jefferson intuitively employed methods of excavation that more than a century later would become standard practice. "I proceeded . . . to make a perpendicular cut through the body of the barrow," he wrote, "that I might examine its internal structure."

Coolly appraising the layers of bone and stone, he reasoned that the mound "has derived both origin and growth from the accustomary collection of bones, and deposition of them together; that the first collection had been deposited on the common surface of the earth, a few stones put over it, and then a covering of earth, that the second had been laid on this . . . and was then also covered with earth; and so on."

By employing just such techniques as Jefferson's, along with modern dating methods, archeologists now know that the mounds—numbering in the tens of thousands—fall into categories as varied as the times and cultures that produced them.

Dirt mounds first rose shortly after 1000 B.C., along what is now the Ohio Valley from Indiana into West Virginia, with some as far east as the Chesapeake Bay region. Archeologists have named the culture that erected them for the great mound excavated in 1902 on the Adena estate near Chillicothe, Ohio. These mounds mark the beginning of the 1,700-year span called the Burial Mound Period. The settled forest life of the builders of these mounds, sustained by hunting, gathering, and some agriculture, archeologists term the Woodland tradition. It would persist in some areas of the East until the coming of the Europeans.

The origin of the Adena way of life stirs continuing discussion. Many authorities think it reaches back to eastern Archaic cultures; others to Middle America—perhaps even to a migration of people from there. However Adena culture began, its central theme was an obsessive preoccupation with death—a cult of the dead—expressed in tall conical mounds and one of the earliest recognizable art styles of native America.

A MOUND in West Virginia's northern panhandle, the Cresap, was in 1958 one of the few Adena mounds left untouched by treasure hunters. Excavation of the small earthen dome revealed a succession of burials that spanned much of Adena history.

During a discussion of the mound its principal excavator, Don W. Dragoo of Pittsburgh's Carnegie Museum, told me, "They apparently chose the site of a house for the burial mound. At the bottom of it we uncovered a specially prepared clay floor 40 feet across and surrounded by a shallow trench."

The first Cresap dead were interred in shallow bark-lined graves, or cremated in fire-reddened clay basins. Soon these were buried beneath a small hump of dirt. Additional burials over the years culminated in a final ceremony, centered on a large fire atop the mound, that marked the last of at least 54 burials. Elsewhere, such successive additions raised Adena mounds to heights that place them among the largest earthworks known. In downtown Moundsville, West

Virginia, the Grave Creek Mound rises to a height of nearly 70 feet.

Archeologists can only speculate on the ceremonies that accompanied the Adena elite to the grave, along with copper jewelry, tubular stone smoking pipes, and polished stone axes and ornaments. Doubtless the rituals were the charge of shamans, or "holy men," for their paraphernalia and costume occasionally come to light in the burial mounds. The remains of an elk-antler headdress lay near one of the Cresap burials, and part of what might have been a squirrel-skin medicine bag came from the Niles-Wolford Mound in Ohio, along with a toothy section of bone cut from the mouth of a wolf. A burial from a Kentucky mound showed the use of this unusual object.

"When we restored the human skull," Raymond S. Baby of the Ohio State Museum told me, "we found that the man's upper front teeth had been removed—and long before death, because the bone had healed over. The wolf-jaw cutout could be inserted into this cavity and manipulated with the tongue. One can imagine the wolf teeth projecting from the medicine man's mouth, and him—perhaps with the skin of a wolf head over his upper face—jumping around, grunting and growling, and making a perfectly good wolf-man."

Stone tablets bearing bird motifs and curvilinear abstractions best show the achievement of the Adena artist. Small enough to fit comfortably in the hand, the tablets may have functioned as stamps for ritual body paint—some still contain red pigment in their deep recesses.

B Y THE SECOND CENTURY B.C. another Woodland culture—Hopewell—had appeared in the Ohio Valley, and its precise relationship to Adena culture, as Baby said to me, "will take years of excavation to resolve." Eventually the Hopewell people took much of the Adena death-cult art style and mound-building practices and carried both to proportions of magnificence.

The largest Hopewell ceremonial center—at Newark, Ohio—held four square miles of interconnected earthworks before modern building activity obliterated most of them. The arrangement was composed of a 26-acre circle joined to an octagon twice its area. A chain of enclosures, walls, and mounds lay more than a mile away. Two avenues between parallel embankments connected the distant clusters; another led to the riverbank, two and a half miles to the south.

To the children's oft-repeated question about ancient peoples, "How did they dress?" the Hopewellians themselves left some answers.

In August 1881 workmen digging a building foundation in West Newark amid the earthworks found a six-inch stone effigy of a seated man, evidently a shaman clad in the whole skin of a bear whose head rested on the man's. In the shaman's lap lay a human head in profile decorated, like his own, with round earspools.

Fragments of textiles, sometimes preserved by contact with copper ornaments in Hopewellian graves, and clay figurines provide more answers. Cloth was dyed red, black, or yellow, and printed with curvilinear designs. From it women made wraparound skirts; the men wore breechcloths. Leather they fashioned into clothing and moccasins, and feathers into blankets or capes. Necklaces were of shell and silver. Some men—probably medicine men like the West Newark figure—wore antler headdresses, teeth, or jawbones of humans or animals.

A trade network that covered much of the United States provided materials for Hopewell artisans. They imported obsidian from Yellowstone and chipped it into thin wide ceremonial blades; copper nuggets from the northern Great Lakes they hammered into embossed breastplates, ear ornaments, or ritual weapons. Mica sheets from the southern Appalachians were cut into silhouettes of hands, bird claws, animals, and headless men; shells from the distant Gulf Coast were fashioned into ornaments or bowls.

This vast trade network carried the unmistakable stamp of the Hopewell death cult to many developing cultures of the Southeast. The Marksville site in central Louisiana looks very much like those in Ohio. Its pottery imitates the incised Hopewell wares. From the Mandeville site in Georgia all the way to Crystal River on the Gulf Coast of Florida searchers have found Hopewell figurines or copper ornaments, along with implements chipped from southern Ohio flint.

Doubtless, the trade was reciprocal, as evidenced by the presence in some of the Ohio sites of pottery decorated in the southern Appalachian technique of stamping the soft clay exterior with wooden paddles carved with checkered, linear, or curved-line motifs.

After about A.D. 550, when the Hopewell way began to fade in the Ohio Valley, Woodland cultures continued to flourish in the Southeast. Some two centuries later a different kind of mound began to rise in its river valleys—the flat-topped platform that characterizes the Temple Mound Period. And a new pattern of life emerged which archeologists call Mississippian, since it may have developed along the Mississippi River. To its people the new tradition meant large villages, intensive corn agriculture, and planting rituals. To archeologists the temple mounds, carefully arranged around spacious plazas, and a myriad of new pottery wares show obvious influences from Middle America. A few miles east of St. Louis, on the Illinois side of the river, the six of us saw the largest Mississippian site of all.

Monks Mound, named for a colony of Trappists who lived nearby in the early 1800's, is the largest prehistoric mound in the United States. Begun around A.D. 900 and completed 250 years later, it dominates the Cahokia site, covering more than 18 acres and rising in great rectangular terraces to a height of 100 feet above the surrounding plain.

On a damp, gray day we scaled the huge mound, climbing a long stepped path bordered by deep gullies, and at times dodging boys who sped shouting down the slope on bicycles. From the summit we saw tree-shaded picnic areas and an occasional mound of the 40 or so in the central part of the site, which is owned and preserved by the State of Illinois. The outer fringes of Cahokia—along with some 200 of its mounds—have become obliterated among the housing developments, trailer camps, and shops that line the highway into Collinsville.

Later we walked or drove to various parts of Cahokia to watch the progress of student crews of the University of Wisconsin-Milwaukee archeological field school. Some worked deep within a low mound, recording cross-sections newly exposed on the high smooth walls of the excavation. Others, in shallow trenches that followed a carefully measured grid, traced the dark stains that marked the post patterns and bastions of successive stages of the great log palisade that centuries ago enclosed the site's center.

Skeleton of a ritual warrior wears traces of the Southern Cult regalia he took to his grave 600 years ago. Unearthed at Georgia's Etowah Mounds, the bones lie mingled with a conch-shell pendant and arm and leg bands of shell beads. An Etowah artisan carved the polished ceremonial ax head and handle from a single piece of slate.

RICHARD SCHLECHT

"There should be a corner near here—to tie into one beyond those trees," one perspiring boy told us. "We'll find it soon."

We paused at the mound excavation before leaving Cahokia and watched students cleaning the smooth floor of the trench. A stain darkened one corner. It reminded me of the first appearance of the tombs we had come across in the same way at Etowah, but we could not stay for the excavation.

Later, at an archeological meeting, I encountered James Anderson, field assistant on the Cahokia project, and asked what they had found. "At least 53 skeletons," was his startling reply, "evidently all female between the ages of 18 and 23. It looks like some sort of sacrifice and burial. That's really all we can say now."

From its unknown origin, Mississippian culture spread rapidly after the 10th century through most of the Southeast—and beyond. Palisaded villages rose along many rivers—Ocmulgee, on central Georgia's Macon Plateau; Moundville, on Alabama's Black Warrior River; the Angel site in southwestern Indiana; and Aztalan, in distant southeastern Wisconsin. Ultimately, the Mississippian way would supplant Woodland culture in the Southeast except for the Middle Atlantic seaboard and extreme southern Florida.

S OMETIME IN THE 14TH CENTURY, perhaps earlier, many southern communities were caught up in a highly ritualistic religion archeologists call the Southern Cult. The area of its concentration more or less follows the line of its known principal centers—Etowah in Georgia; Moundville, Alabama; and Spiro, Oklahoma—but remains of the cult occur from the northern Mississippi Valley to Florida.

In the fall of 1933 the Craig Mound, a tall conical hump of earth with three smaller connecting mounds, stood with six others in a cultivated field beside the Arkansas River, near Spiro, Oklahoma. That November, six unemployed local men, calling themselves the "Pocola Mining Company," signed a two-year lease with the property owner and began a tragic commercial venture. Deaf to the pleadings of archeologists, the diggers pitted and tunneled the Spiro mounds, trundled out in wheelbarrows what archeologists later would term "one of the most amazing caches of ceremonial material ever found in the mound area," and sold most objects on the spot. Others, like a partially mummified body wearing a tasseled headdress of woven straw, they left on a dirt pile to disintegrate. By the fall of 1935 little was left of the site.

"I went out to look at it," archeologist Forrest E. Clements later wrote. "Sections of cedar poles lay scattered on the ground, fragments of feather and fur textiles littered the whole area; it was impossible to take a single step in hundreds of square yards around the ruined structure without scuffing up broken pieces of pottery, sections of engraved shell, and beads of shell, stone, and bone. The site was abandoned; the diggers had completed their work."

An inventory of surviving Spiro artifacts scattered in private collections and museums throughout the country taken some years later by Mr. and Mrs. Henry W. Hamilton of the Missouri Archaeological Society revealed the full extent of the sack of the site. The remarkable loot included 120 or more pipes, 23 of them effigies of humans or animals; 11 human figures carved of cedar, and more than 40 cedar masks;

Indian of the Ohio Adena
culture carries a rabbit past
more successful hunters who
have brought home a deer.
These early dwellers of the
eastern woodlands devoted
themselves largely to honoring the dead with burial
mounds. Their circular
houses, roofed with bark or
thatch, had walls of woven
saplings bound to posts.

RICHARD SCHLECHT, AFTER R. W. LANG IN DON
W. DRAGOO, "MOUNDS FOR THE DEAD," 1963

50 chipped maces or "swords"; nearly 200 conch-shell bowls engraved with intricate mythological scenes and religious motifs.

Spiro art epitomizes the Southern Cult. The shells bear repeated representations of stylized god-animals, including birds or bird-men; plumed, winged, or horned rattlesnakes; and some catlike animals. Ceremonial objects common to the major cult centers include embossed copper gorgets or plates; monolithic axes, batonlike maces, and thin ritual flints—"weapons," wrote the late Antonio J. Waring, Jr., a leading authority on the cult, "whose very fragility must have endowed them with a sort of magical power." Throughout the whole cult area some symbols repeat insistently—sun circles, crosses, and the puzzling bilobed arrow, pointed dartlike designs flanked by semicircular lobes.

The peak of the Southern Cult—and indeed that of the Mississippian culture—had passed shortly before Hernando de Soto crossed the Southeast between 1539 and 1541. A continuation of the old ceremonialism, however, may have been at least partially represented by the Green Corn Ceremony, or Busk, seen by Europeans among the 18th-century Creeks and Cherokees. A ritual of renewal, the Busk ushered in the Creek new year. The Indians first smashed their pottery and quenched old fires. Then they kindled a "new fire" symbolically derived from the sun's heat and fed by four logs laid to form a cross.

The four summers that Gene and I spent helping excavate the cult burials at Etowah were among the most memorable of our lives. Mound C, where I worked, yielded 75 burials during those seasons, many of them in large log tombs. In the museum since built beside the remnants of Etowah's now-grassy moat, we showed the children the cult paraphernalia recovered from Mound C. One plate of embossed copper portrays an eagle-man or hawk-man in a style archeologists long thought represented gods; many of the Etowah tombs, however, contained human bodies dressed in exactly the same way, even to such details as the beaded forelock that dangles over the eyes, and the conch-shell pendant suspended from a necklace of huge shell beads.

I pointed out a copper-covered wooden rattle in the shape of a jawless head and resembling that held by the bird-being on the plate. Bits of a bright copper-studded feather headdress from another tomb recalled the narrative of the meeting somewhere in Louisiana of de Soto with a chieftain and his retinue of "a hundred noblemen, all very magnificently arrayed . . . in large feather headdresses and beautiful robes of marten skin and other much esteemed fur."

A museum silhouette suggests a great temple such as might have topped the mounds at Etowah. De Soto had visited a similar structure somewhere near the Savannah River, not far east of Etowah in the province of Cofachiqui, a name preserved for us by his chroniclers.

"Now this temple was large, being more than a hundred feet in length and forty in width. Its walls were high . . . and its roof also was very lofty and drafty. . . . Over the roof of the temple many large and small shells of different marine animals had been arranged. . . . These shells had been placed with the inside out so as to show their greatest luster, and they included many conch shells of strange magnificence. Between them, spaces had been left . . . and in these spaces were large strands (some of pearls and some of seed pearls) half a fathom in length which hung from the roof and descended in a graduated manner so that where some left off others began. The temple was covered on the outside with all these things, and they made a splendid sight in the brilliance of the sun."

THE ETOWAH MUSEUM holds what is perhaps the most important discovery made at the site: two statues of polished Georgia marble—one a man seated cross-legged; the other a woman with legs drawn under her. The figures, about two feet high, lean slightly forward and stare straight ahead. The headdress of the male includes a coil, perhaps of hair, on the back of the head; that of the female is a low flat cap with a ridge leading down to an object like a knapsack on her back. Both statues bear red, white, green, and black paint that defines vestlike garments and details the eyes and mouths.

No one knows the function of the statues, but de Soto provides a possible clue. In the mortuary temple he visited on the Savannah River, he saw wooden chests containing bodies, and "a yard above each of them was a statue carved from wood and placed on a pedestal against the wall. This was a personal likeness of the man or woman within the chest and was made at the age he or she had attained at death. Thus these likenesses served as memorials for the deceased."

De Soto also met the lovely mistress of the province of Cofachiqui. She presented him with a "large strand of pearls as thick as hazelnuts which encircled her neck three times and fell to her thighs," and de Soto bestowed upon her a Spanish ring of gold, set with a ruby, "as a symbol of the peace and friendship they were discussing." Unfortunately, her realm could not endure. Europeans came in greater and greater numbers, and the magnificence of life along the southern rivers, already in decline, disappeared altogether.

Mica hand glistens after centuries of burial in an Ohio Hopewell mound. Emerging in the second century B.C. and surviving until about A.D. 550, the Hopewell culture shaped a profusion of human, animal, and geometric figure cut from sheets of mica.

OHIO HISTORICAL SOCIETY, COLUMBUS

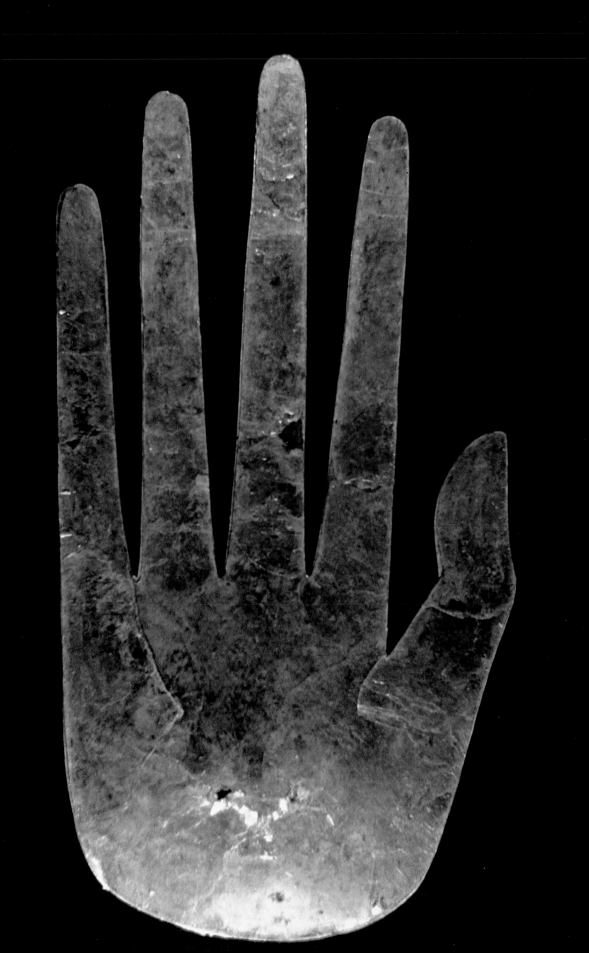

GREAT SERPENT MOUND AND COPPER HAWK EVOKE OHIO'S PAST

Largest known serpent-effigy mound in the world, the 1,254-foot monster below uncoils atop a bluff in southern Ohio. Paths for visitors enclose the reptile's 20-foot-wide body. Giant loops extend from whorled tail (left) to gaping mouth. The significance of the oval clasped in the jaws—possibly an egg or a frog—remains a mystery. One of many earthen animal effigies in the United States, the sinuous mound exemplifies American Indian ritual artifacts that express veneration of wild creatures. Since serpents also figured prominently in the religions and mythologies of ancient Egypt, Assyria, and Greece, some 19th-century scholars believed that peoples from the Old World had created this effigy. But characteristic artifacts and a house site found in nearby burial mounds have since indicated Adena people as the builders. Now a state memorial, the effigy once lay open to curiosity seekers, who found it barren of antiquities. In 1887 an archeologist restored sections damaged by digging, following a survey of 1848. Hopewell people, as well as

the earlier Adena, inhabited this part of Ohio. Both cultures conducted cremations and burials inside wooden buildings, then burned the mortuaries and covered them with earth to form mounds. Hopewell burial offerings, however, far surpassed those of the Adena. Surrounded by finely wrought art objects like the hammered copper hawk at right, the Hopewell elite often went to their graves arrayed in pearl-embroidered costumes. Simple bone cups and copper beads, and stone blades and points, accompanied the Adena dead.

J. W. DYER (OPPOSITE) AND W. T. AUSTIN

SALTS CAVE, EERIE PASSAGEWAY TO PREHISTORY

Torchlight opens the craggy corridors of Salts Cave, Mammoth Cave Park, Kentucky, to the inspection of "action archeology" volunteers of the Cave Research Foundation who simulate aboriginal exploration methods. Indians roaming the cave more than 2,000 years ago left behind similar cane-and-weed torches. The volunteer above tastes mirabilite, a salty mineral possibly used by the prehistoric people of the area both as a condiment and a cathartic. They also mined gypsum, perhaps to make white paint or plaster. Below, explorers nourish a fire with cane fuel in the manner of the ancient miners. Archeologists deduced this technique from the many fagots discarded there by the Indians. Analysis of prehistoric human fecal deposits indicates the cave Indians cultivated much of their food—a milestone in dating their transition from hunting and foraging to farming. The National Geographic Society provided financial assistance for investigations here.

MARTIN ROGERS

SCIENCE AND INDUSTRY COOPERATE TO PROTECT THE REMNANTS OF AN ANCIENT VILLAGE

Field near Atlanta, Georgia, abounds with postholes outlining the floors of circular houses dating between A.D. 1 and 500. The Great Southwest Corporation began clearing this tract in 1968 for an industrial park. Alerted to the value of the debris and pocked subsurface by an amateur archeologist, the corporation immediately postponed construction work here, made the site available for careful excavation, and provided money and equipment. At left, a front-end loader clears away earth dug by students who joined in baring the house patterns with shovels and trowels—even brooms.

Dark centers of the circles above indicate hearths; the blackened crater of a cooking pit appears at upper left. Student volunteers in the right foreground work at uncovering another floor. In the tree-shaded area to their left they opened a large pit containing a pottery human figurine and fragments of charred bone —some animal, others possibly human. A University of Georgia team headed by Arthur R. Kelly, Joseph R. Caldwell, and Lawrence Meier has unearthed the traces of more than two dozen structures here, as well as excavating a score of cooking and storage pits.

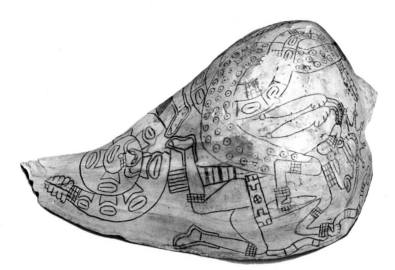

BUILDERS OF MOUNDS LEFT A HAUNTING RECORD ON SHELL, STONE, AND WOOD

Indian works of art reflect the richness of prehistoric religion over 15 centuries in the eastern United States. Much of the symbolism defies interpretation today. At Spiro, Oklahoma, a great 14th-century Southern Cult ceremonial center, artists engraved intricate designs on conch shells. Entwined rattlesnakes join together the bodies of two dancing men who circle the foot-long shell above. Archeologists believe the bubble issuing from the mouth of the visible figure represents a speech scroll. He wears a crownlike headdress with a long forelock ornament, earspools, a choker collar, a belt with a cross motif, arm and leg bands, and moccasins. Similar ornaments appear on the male heads and dancing bird-man shown on the shell rubbings below. Lines band eyes and cheeks to form the "weeping eye," a characteristic of Southern Cult art, possibly indicating face painting. The antlered cedar mask with shell inlays (opposite, right) also came from the Spiro mounds. An excavation in 1901 near Chillicothe, Ohio, unearthed the stone pipe at right. Carved two millenniums ago by an Adena craftsman, it represents one of the finest known examples of their art style.

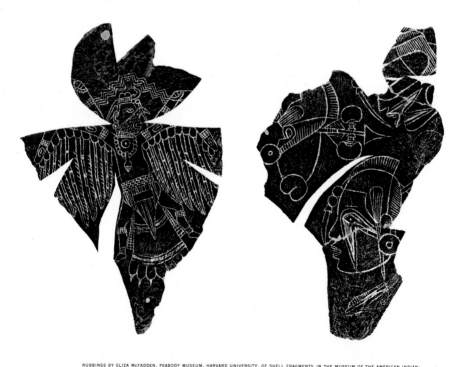

CENTURIES LIE ENTOMBED IN MOUNDS

Communing with the past, the Stuarts stroll across a 600-year-old mound beside the Etowah River in Georgia. Indians of the late prehistoric era built earthen platforms here to hold temples and chieftains' houses and established a village with a protective moat. Archeologists digging into the flank of Mound B (above) found refuse from countless feasts—turtle shells, deer and fish bones, and even human bone fragments blackened and broken in a manner suggesting cannibalism. The site also held

GORDON W. GAHAN (BELOW); LYNTHA SCOTT EILER (ABOVE);
GEORGE E. STUART, N.G.S. STAFF, ETOWAH MUSEUM, ETOWAH, GEORGIA

evidence of habitation by later Indians, who avoided as sacred the ground of an adjacent mound. The summit temple may have resembled the one built by Mississippian people at Moundville, Alabama, and reconstructed (right) by archeologists using typical posthole patterns as guides. Another Etowah mound yielded a rich store of Southern Cult burials and art, like the necklace and shell gorget at left, showing a ceremonially dressed figure holding aloft a fragile ritual sword of flint.

151

INDIAN ART EXPRESSES REVERENCE FOR BOTH THE NATURAL AND THE SUPERNATURAL

'In form, or mere contour, it portrayed with startling fidelity and delicacy, the head of a young deer or doe, a little under life-size," wrote Frank H. Cushing, discoverer of the 370-year-old effigy at left. Finest of many wooden sculptures recovered in 1895 from a mangrove swamp at Key Marco, Florida, it once had tortoiseshell eyes; its ears moved at the twitch of a string. Crea-

tures of seashell leap among disks surrounding a human figure on the two deerskins below, fashioned by Virginia Indians in the early 17th century. Knotted horned rattlesnakes and hand-and-eye motif of the Southern Cult decorate the engraved 12-inch stone disk (above) unearthed at Moundville, Alabama; it may have served as a palette for applying body paint.

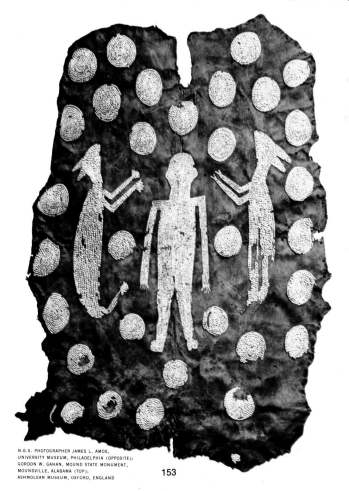

N.G.S. PHOTOGRAPHER JAMES L. AMOS,
UNIVERSITY MUSEUM, PHILADELPHIA (OPPOSITE);
GORDON W. GAHAN, MOUND STATE MONUMENT,
MOUNDVILLE, ALABAMA (TOP);
ASHMOLEAN MUSEUM, OXFORD, ENGLAND

Aboriginal traditions mingle with European influences in this mid-19th-century painting of a Louisiana Cho

e. The Indians continue basketry and weaving, but clothing and iron kettles reflect Old World encroachments.

6

SOUTH AMERICA

A vast continent forms a varied stage for peoples ranging from the fishers of Tierra del Fuego to the empire-building Incas of the Andes

"THE AGE WILL COME, in the ripeness of time," wrote Seneca the Roman philosopher, "when Ocean will loosen the chain of things and bare new worlds to the storms. Then a huge country will be revealed and Thule will no longer be the last land."

The Thule that Seneca referred to was the end of the Roman world, somewhere on the fog-shrouded shores of northern Europe; the "country" he so prophetically imagined—the lands of the Western Hemisphere—would not take definite shape on maps for 15 centuries.

In the decades of exploitation that followed their arrival in the New World, Spanish adventurers conquered part of the hemisphere's northern half, then turned to the southern continent—a land as vast and varied as the one they already knew.

The Andes, longest mountain chain in the world, shapes the 4,500-mile western edge of South America into giant ice-capped corrugations that include the 42 highest peaks in the Western Hemisphere. Inland from the curve of the northern mountains, in a distance that varies between 50 and 300 miles, the land drops abruptly into steaming jungle etched by rivers that fall from these heights and from the highlands of Venezuela and Brazil to feed the Amazon River in its long search for the Atlantic. Southward, the jungle gradually gives way to drier lowland, then to the open reaches of Patagonia—a narrow world of grassland that stretches all the way to the continent's cold, windswept tip.

Near the ancient city of Chan Chan, a Peruvian tends his rock-weighted crab trap. Archeologists believe his pre-Columbian ancestors plied the sea in reed boats like those upended in the foreground, but as yet know little about such South Americans as the Nazcas who shaped the 7-inch effigy bottle above.

DAVID BRILL (OPPOSITE) AND VICTOR R. BOSWELL, JR., N.G.S. STAFF, COURTESY ALAN R. SAWYER

When Seneca made his prophecy, around the time of Christ, man had already occupied that southernmost cape for 9,000 years. In A.D. 1532, in another part of the continent, Spaniards found the highest achievement of man's long stay: the Inca Empire—an expression of civilization fully as dazzling as that their countrymen had marveled at in the high interior of Mexico.

What took place in South America between the Ice Age and the time of the Incas, I knew, was a complex and elusive story, wrought in part by the size and variety of the land and for most of the continent little-known in detail.

"Each bit of archeology in South America is like a tiny gleam of light on a vast dark landscape," Alan R. Sawyer remarked to Gene and me one morning in his office at the Textile Museum in Washington, D. C. "The situation is much like man's first walk on the moon in relation to the whole surface. Thus, we can speak of the happenings of prehistory only in generalities."

This is particularly true of the lands east of the Andes, where the trowel and shovel have revealed no more than sporadic glimpses of prehistoric life that vaguely sketch the general movements of peoples and cultures. As one travels into the mountainous areas of the north-western part of the continent, the monuments of the high cultures centered in Peru become increasingly evident; yet many of these remain to this day only spectacular and enigmatic landmarks of the past.

T HE SOUTHLANDS, where a thick matting of grass prevented farming, helped mold man into fisher, hunter of guanaco or ostrich, or gatherer of seeds and roots. When Europeans arrived, they found the Ona, Yahgan, and other primitive peoples in the interior and along the coastlines still living by these simple skills.

In the arid desert country where Argentina, Bolivia, and Chile meet lie puzzling ruins that date from the late prehistoric period—the centuries after A.D. 700. The mesas and plateaus, the dry washes and the vegetation of that area bear a distinct resemblance to those of the North American Southwest—and so do some of the cultural remains. Here, I learned, agricultural desert dwellers built, in succession, pit houses, rectangular stone structures, and, finally, clustered compounds of as many as 250 rooms. The remarkable similarity between the widely separated areas extends to basketry, geometric pottery decoration, copper bells, and stone artifacts.

"Many of these items are not just similar," archeologist Betty J. Meggers told me. "They are virtually identical. But there are good arguments against direct cultural contact: First, many of the traits occur in the intervening high-culture areas, and could have diffused independently north and south; second, contact would have had to continue over several centuries without affecting the adjacent coastal areas. Similar environments and raw materials appear mainly responsible for the parallel development."

Betty Meggers and her husband Clifford Evans, both of the Smithsonian Institution, are among the relatively few archeologists who have worked in the vastness of the Amazon Basin. Their project in 1948 took them by airplane, steamer, and dugout to Marajó Island just south of the Amazon River Delta, where they excavated jungle sites

*"New and most exact description of America or the fourth part of the
world," reads the Latin inscription on this map engraved in 1652 and
showing the extent of European exploration along the coasts and rivers
of Central and South America. The continent appears in remarkably accurate
outline. Cartographers gave the Amazon a serpentine form; figures above
"Gigantum Regio," near the tip, betray a belief in a "Kingdom of Giants."*

that revealed a picture of life in the Brazilian forest as it was between 1000 B.C. and European contact.

"Rain and humidity in such a place present problems," Evans told me, "not only because of the physical discomfort involved, but also because of the destructive effect on the archeological material. Moisture and heat have combined to obliterate many of the remains that might survive in other areas."

Despite such difficulties, the couple found refuse deposits that yielded evidence of villages—some consisting of a single large communal house of wattle and daub—where 100 to 150 people lived a settled life based on hunting and fishing, and perhaps some agriculture. The depth of the refuse and the uniformity of the stratified remains within it indicate that the settlements might have enjoyed a hundred years or so of quiet existence, apparently undisturbed by others. Pottery, one of the best-preserved time markers in the human story, reached this side of South America around 1000 B.C., perhaps from the west where the New World's earliest dated pottery—3000 B.C. —has been found on the coasts of Colombia and Ecuador.

The story of man to the northwest, in the Venezuela area, I discovered, is one of movement and displacement that ultimately affected the peopling of islands of the Caribbean.

Excavation of sites along the northern reaches of the Orinoco River, where the alluvial delta begins to stretch fingering streams toward the Atlantic, shows that just before the birth of Christ invaders drove out the manioc-farming ancestors of the Arawaks. Moving north, the displaced people eventually migrated into the West Indies sometime before A.D. 300. There they found a simple fishing people—the Ciboney —who had come out of Venezuela centuries earlier.

Last to arrive in the West Indies were the warlike Caribs. According to their traditions, they invaded the Lesser Antilles at their southern end shortly before the time of Columbus, killing off the Arawak men and taking the women as wives. The Ciboney by then had retreated into western Haiti and Cuba.

Thus was the stage set for the landfall of Columbus, who reported seeing "both men and women go as naked as they were born."

O F MAINLAND SOUTH AMERICA'S mysterious remains, none intrigue me so much as the large stone figures that lie scattered by the hundreds among overgrown mounds at some 30 major sites outside the modern village of San Agustín, not far from the headwaters of the Magdalena River in the Andean highlands of southwestern Colombia.

In 1932, having translated the report by German archeologist Konrad Theodor Preuss on some of the figures, Hermann von Walde-Waldegg of the University of Bogotá made his first reconnaissance journey to the area. He reported later, ". . . my eyes lighted upon something that almost made me fall off my horse. . . . in the dirt and grass of a meadow lay two heavy figures of carved stone. . . . Each was about as tall as a man. With their long jaguar eyeteeth and broad noses, they looked like something out of a nightmare, but to me as an archeologist they were infinitely beautiful."

During two seasons von Walde-Waldegg excavated 142 additional

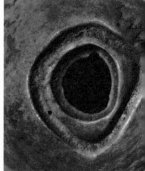

Indian surgeons twice trepanned this centuries-old skull from Bolivia, using instruments like the delicate copper celts above. The earlier, larger incision partially healed, indicating a successful first operation. Trepanning relieved pressure from fractures or, as some cultures believed, released demons.

statues, as well as several temples and many tombs. Subsequent finds doubled the number of figures.

I found the size of some of the stone giants amazing. Some weigh more than 15 tons; one measures 21½ feet high. Many, with their exaggerated heads and squat bodies, stand rigidly in San Agustín's Archeological Park. Some are snouted, others bare the overlapping fangs of the feline, and most hold objects — maces, carved shields, or trophy heads. Some appear as man-alligators, snakes, or serpent-eating eagles, and many are bedecked in jewelry and wearing loincloths or skirts.

In the course of digging — both by archeologists and by treasure hunters — the earthen mounds in the area of the mountain village have yielded temples, rectangular slab tombs, and coffins carved from large blocks of stone. Some of the hollowed stones serve present-day inhabitants of San Agustín as horse-watering troughs or as vessels in which to ferment corn for making *chicha*, the Andean beer.

San Agustín's remarkable remains have themselves impeded the solution of the mystery of their origin. "The search for more statues and temples," lamented Gerardo Reichel-Dolmatoff of Bogotá's University of the Andes, "has, at times, obscured the main problems of stratigraphy and typology, and even now, after years of digging, the major questions of origins, chronology, and external relationships are largely a matter for conjecture."

The sites have yielded a single radiocarbon reading of 500 B.C., in what appears from related stratigraphy to be the earliest date in a developmental span of 1,500 years. No one knows the place and significance of the statues in the long sequence.

If San Agustín remains a mystery, so do the burial chambers in the Tierradentro region of the mountainous Department of Cauca to the north. Spiral staircases, once concealed beneath ground-level slabs, lead downward to eerie rooms carved out of the soft bedrock. Oval or circular in plan, and sometimes interrupted by columns and niches, the chambers bear painted parallel lines, concentric diamond shapes, circles, and occasional human faces in red, white, black, and yellow — decorations that cover virtually every inch of space. Urns, once set into wall niches or floor pits, contained the remains of people as little-understood today as those of San Agustín, for they have yet to be dated or studied in detail.

In Peru — which to the archeologist includes the fringes of bordering Ecuador, Bolivia, and Chile — more excavation has been carried out than in all the rest of South America combined. But despite careful excavations around the turn of the century by the father of Peruvian archeology, Max Uhle, and the dedicated work of many others, uncounted ruins remain untouched, appearing only as tantalizing patterns in the jumbled terrain of the highlands and in the succession of short valleys that cut across Peru's narrow coastal desert. Common to most of the ruins, though, are craters left by the *huaquero*, or treasure hunter — the modern counterpart of the Spanish gold seeker — who finds a ready market for the artifacts of precious metal or pottery and the textiles that he occasionally comes upon.

"Lamentably, fully 99 percent of the Peruvian artifacts you will see in the world's museums or in private collections," Alan Sawyer told us, "come from the work of the huaqueros. The antiquities laws are, unfortunately, not enforceable—especially in remote areas. Add this to the natural desire of people to lift themselves out of poverty, and you have the explanation of the situation."

The treasures of art that come from the land span some 3,000 years, for civilization sprang up in Peru sometime in the second millennium B.C. in a broad setting of sedentary village life and a vigorous population that possessed pottery, the loom, and considerable architectural skill. The time was one of increasing corn agriculture and, possibly, the rise of the first ceremonial centers. Many archeologists refer to this era as the Initial Period. From this time forward the saga of Peru is one of cults and cultures whose remains archeologists are just now beginning to sift in earnest. Some ancient peoples, they find, probably developed in the isolation afforded by the abrupt barriers of mountain or desert, while others forged stronger patterns of culture that diffused over wide areas of highland and coast.

"This rise, spread, and fall of peoples can be likened to the blinking of lights on a computer panel," one archeologist told me. "Depending on the time within the last 3,000 years of Peruvian prehistory, the lights would blink on and off, seemingly at random; at other times clusters of lights appear with the rise of influential kingdoms or states; and—rarely—the whole board glows with the spread of religion or military empire."

Archeologists have varying methods for segmenting man's past in Peru. Some use stages of development, others time periods. But stages —the labeled giant steps of cultural progress—have often proved awkward, since human development did not follow simultaneously a regular pattern over the whole land.

Of the many systems in current use I prefer the one that simply divides the time after 1800 B.C. into six convenient spans—the Initial Period, 1800 to 900 B.C., followed by Early, Middle, and Late Horizons separated by two Intermediate Periods.

The Early Horizon, lasting from about 900 to 200 B.C., was marked by the sudden peak of the jaguar-obsessed Chavín cult and the rapid spread of its art style over much of Peru. Artistry of another sort, in the talented hands of craftsmen of the Nazca and Mochica peoples, reached a zenith at opposite ends of the coast during the Early Intermediate Period, 200 B.C. to A.D. 600. The Middle Horizon, A.D. 600 to 1000, witnessed the rise of Peru's first empire, centered at the city of Huari in the central highlands. The Late Intermediate Period, A.D. 1000 to the 1470's, was a time between empires, an era of small highland states and larger coastal kingdoms like that of the Chimú people. Situated on the north coast, the Chimú kingdom flourished until conquered by the Incas, whose period of greatness defines the Late Horizon. This endured until 1533, when subjects of the Inca Empire heaped a stone-walled room in Cajamarca with gold and silver in a futile attempt to ransom their emperor from the conqueror Francisco Pizarro.

Geographically, the story of the civilizations of Peru might begin at any one of many sites. Perhaps it could start with the great coastal temple at the ceremonial center of La Florida in Lima, unexcavated but dated around 1800 B.C., or at Kotosh, 150 miles away on the eastern fringe of the Andes, where archeologists from the University of Tokyo have dated one stage of its temple at 1450 B.C., but this Initial Period is yet an obscure era. I would prefer to start at the site of Chavín de Huantar, whose principal temple was begun around 900 B.C.

Its large rectangular temple complex and sunken plaza nestle on the eastern side of the continental divide, 140 miles north of Lima and some 10,000 feet higher than that sea-level capital. In the small Mosna Valley, a side pocket of the Marañon Valley which bisects the northern Andes, silence fills the sacred riverside center, and sunlight sparkles on the cold stone. Inside the oldest portion of the main temple, in the dim half-light where two passageways cross, stands a vertical shaft almost 15 feet high, carved in the image of the principal deity of the Chavín cult to which the site gives its name.

This tall, bulging stone bears the grinning fanged countenance of a man-jaguar with serpents representing hair. The shaft, adorned with a rich intertwining of strange symbolic scrolls, is surmounted by successive partial profiles of fanged faces, and the whole still exerts a power—"an awe-inspiring quality," as University of California archeologist John H. Rowe once put it, "which can be felt even by a present day unbeliever."

That quality apparently was appreciated some 2,800 years ago when the dynamic Chavín religion—with motifs including the jaguar, the serpent, the bird of prey, and an alligator-like form—welded for half a millennium the first unity among the ancient cultures of Peru. The great burst of the Chavín cult, archeologists estimate, took place between 900 and 800 B.C.

Eternally poised for battle, a Mochica soldier personifies the warlike culture of his creator. Ceramists unsurpassed in ancient Peru, the Mochicas dominated the Moche and Chicama Valleys of the north coast from 200 B.C. to A.D. 600. Realistic clay portraits and painted scenes help archeologists reconstruct everyday Mochica life.

C HAVÍN DESIGNS including bold curvilinear heads of humans, felines, and birds of prey decorate the burnished black bottles from the coastal site of Cupisnique, 180 air miles northwest of Chavín de Huantar. For several centuries at least the Chavín influence was reflected in the brilliant resin-painted vessels of the Paracas culture, 200 miles to the south. The full influence of the Chavín cult, in architecture, ceramics, and textiles, covered much of Peru.

The origin of the Chavín cult remains one of the great unresolved questions of Peruvian archeology. Some believe its roots lie in Peru's north coast, others in the northern highlands; still others see an early form of Chavín monumental art in the toothy features and distorted anatomy of the figures on the row of monoliths at yet-undated Cerro Sechín, on the coast roughly west of Chavín de Huantar.

Peruvian scholar Julio C. Tello was first to carry out a thorough study at Chavín de Huantar and to define the great extent of the influence of its cult. He believed its beginnings lay in the lowland jungle just east of the Andes.

"And I agree," Alan Sawyer told us. "The jaguar and alligator of Chavín art are jungle animals, not native to the mountains. Until we know more of that jungle to the east, we shouldn't conclude that the origins lie elsewhere."

Yale archeologist Michael Coe would trace the art to another jungle, in distant Mexico. "It might well have started there," he told me. "We know that when Olmec civilization flourished in Mexico—around 1200 B.C.—a long-range maritime trade network probably existed between the Pacific coast of Middle America and Ecuador. Certainly this route easily could have been extended to reach Peru. Considering the parallels in the art, I personally think it could have happened."

Chavín de Huantar itself seems to be the largest of the cult centers and the most elaborate. Its temple complex—the so-called Castillo and its successive additions—measures about 250 feet wide and twice as long, and dominates the ruin. Ramps and stairways connect its three levels of rooms, and airshafts still ventilate some of the interior chambers, though many remain filled with the rubble of collapsed masonry. An elaborate system of underground passageways honeycombs the site, and some, I heard with surprise, may lead beneath the river to the other side.

Most archeologists believe the small Mosna Valley could not have supported a large permanent population. They think Chavín de Huantar was not actually a city but essentially a religious center where priests served the deities in near-empty temples most of the year while awaiting seasonal pilgrimages by peoples of the settlements scattered over the countryside.

WITH IMAGINATION, reinforced by some archeological evidence, you might visualize a family of Chavín times preparing for their pilgrimage to the distant center in the Mosna Valley. Leaving their small thatched stone house in the chill dawn, they fill their llama's pack with corn, dehydrated potatoes, and dried meat—some for use during encampment at the center, the rest perhaps as offerings to the priests.

Through the early morning fog they file—the mother and father, three small children bundled against the cold wind, and the surefooted llama. The parents chew narcotic coca to lessen the effects of fatigue and chill. The trail, studded with slippery rocks, grows steep and narrow, then dips to meet another path. There, perhaps, the family is joined by distant neighbors seldom seen except on these journeys into the tiny valley of religion. The same narrow path trod by Chavín pilgrims can be seen today, winding up the side of a mountain until it disappears into the clouds.

The concept of the ceremonial center, I have found, is certainly an early one over much of ancient America. It may well have characterized the activity of the Chavín cult until the power of its gods waned between 500 and 200 B.C.

Some 170 miles south of Lima the sun-bleached Paracas Peninsula makes a hilly bulge on Peru's south coast. The half-buried ruin that overlooks one of the bays sheltered by the peninsula is sandy, windswept, and dreary, but to this place in 1925 Julio Tello traced some ancient textiles that had appeared on the illegal market. Within the foundations of a stone building he came upon one of the most spectacular finds ever made by an archeologist in Peru.

The dusty dry fill of the Paracas Necropolis, the burial-ground site of Tello's discovery, yielded an incredible deposit of more than 400 large bundles. Each contained a desiccated body tightly wrapped in alternating layers of plain cotton and, in profusion, rich garments that included some of the finest examples of the embroiderer's art that any age of man has produced.

Among the folds of the brilliantly embroidered mantles, ponchos, multicolored shirts, turbans, and bags lay more offerings—ornaments

Crudely carved animal decorates a wall in Cuzco, the Inca capital. Excelling as builders and engineers, the Incas cut stone blocks to exact dimensions and positioned them without mortar.

of gold, weapons, pottery, and woven-cane fans fringed with feathers — as many as 150 such artifacts in a single mummy bundle. The Necropolis cache dates from the second century B.C. or shortly afterward, and reflects the remarkable tradition of the Paracas craftsmen.

Gene and I once examined an example of late-Paracas weaving in the Brooklyn Museum in New York—a rectangular mantle covered by geometric face designs and fringed with three-dimensional figures made by the rare "needle-knit" technique. The effigies that remain appear to be knitted, but the Paracas master craftsman actually fashioned them with a single needle and lengths of colored yarn over a padding base of cotton or yarn. On this particular piece some 90 figures—men, plants, and animals—take form in vivid color. The miniature men wear fringed shirts, breechcloths, kilts, or fanlike headdresses; some brandish war clubs; even the llama appears, perhaps a sacrificial animal.

In the centuries just before the birth of Christ, the influence of the Chavín cult faded, and other peoples began to make their mark on a new age that saw the beginnings of militarism. One, the Nazca, dwelt south of the Paracas Peninsula; another, the Mochica, lived in the Moche Valley nearly 600 miles to the northwest.

The Nazca Valley, one of a converging series in the south-coast desert, gives its name not only to the people who inhabited the area and conquered neighboring peoples, but to the famed "Nazca Lines" that rank high among the mysteries of New World prehistory.

On the desert plateau that overlooks the Nazca Valley, there appears from the air a complex geometrical explosion etched into the dry yellow sand—so vast that it dwarfs to near-oblivion the thin dark ribbon of the Pan American Highway that cuts across part of it. Arrow-straight lines or tapering bands—some nearly five miles long—crisscross complex patterns of triangles, trapezoids, spirals, zigzags, and intricate distorted effigies of birds and animals. Undiscovered—or unappreciated—until the age of flight, this desert geometry remains a puzzle. Some believe that many of the markings formed sighting lines of astronomical significance, but a 1968 study by astronomer Gerald Hawkins, sponsored in part by the National Geographic Society, revealed no clear correlation between the mysterious configurations and the movements of the stars and planets. One member of his expedition called the flat sweep of gravel-covered desert containing the lines "the world's largest scratch pad."

The Nazcas themselves achieved a kind of immortality in their ceramic arts. "The emergence of the vital Nazca style," Alan Sawyer told us, "seems to reflect a dynamic new religion in the south—one that unified the peoples of its valleys for the first time."

Nazca pottery occasionally gives us views of life's smaller moments: Fishermen ride inflated animal skins; farmers chase birds from their fields; and a one-man band sits busily engrossed in playing panpipes, horn, rattle, and drum. Religious motifs so common on Nazca pottery often show stylized animals—birds, killer whales—or effigies of humans carrying trophy heads. Warm, earthy colors dominate these compositions. I have counted as many as 14 appearing in rich harmony on a single vessel; the Nazcas were masters of polychrome pottery.

Pottery, as Gene and the children and I saw amply demonstrated

Conqueror of Peru, Francisco Pizarro in the 1530's wrested a rich empire from the Incas, who had ruled the Andean highlands and the arid coast for less than a century.

throughout our travels, is one of the archeologist's most valuable clues to the past. Its initial plasticity makes it sensitive to man's clever hands and the changing whim of fad or fashion, and its fired hardness renders it—aside from stone and gold—the most lasting and durable of materials. Like the changes in car styling that might someday provide an archeologist with a properly stratified junk pile, the subtle or sudden changes in pottery excavated in sequence can reflect tangible evidence of ancient cultural change, trade, or influence. The remarkable Mochica pottery, like that of the Nazca, does even more in allowing us a glimpse of the people themselves living out their lives—a rare privilege in the archeology of Peru.

"I almost feel that I know them," Ann marveled one evening as she studied page after page of pictures of Mochica vessels. The incredibly talented artists had molded and modeled and painted uniformed warriors in full battle readiness, merchants lugging wares on their bent backs, prisoners of war bound with ropes, mothers with children, and even people at work with looms inside a textile factory. Some vessels portray individuals; others provide the setting for the small figures painted on their surface.

On one jar two men approach the end of their climb up the narrow surface of a ramp that spirals around the vessel. One of them carries bags of beans to a figure seated in a miniature building. The other holds ceremonial wands, possibly used in divination.

THE FREQUENT APPEARANCE of soldiers in Mochica art reflects the importance of the military in the people's lives. At times the fighting men march briskly in file, the troops clad in turbans and conical helmets with chin straps, and bearing war clubs. Higher ranks rate headdresses of birds, feathers, or animal heads, but all wear uniforms of belted tunics much like those of the Roman legions an ocean away. All have lower legs painted as if wearing high boots. One soldier in a spiked helmet gestures an order, his arm out-thrust and his mouth wide open and drawn into a snarl. The scene may depict an actual event—troops mounting an attack on a neighboring valley, or defending their own towns and fields against an aggressor.

Archeology has helped give a fuller picture of the events behind such military scenes. Many of the skulls unearthed in Mochica burials contain circular holes, witness to frequent instances of trepanning—surgery that removed bone and relieved the pressure of mace-inflicted head wounds. Evidence of Mochica invasion overlies the debris of cultures as distant as the Nepeña Valley, nearly 100 miles south of the Moche Valley homeland. The motive for the attacks? Possibly lack of arable land. The monumental study of Virú Valley settlement patterns undertaken by archeologist Gordon R. Willey indicates that coastal populations reached a peak just before Mochica times—a factor of no small importance when you consider that only narrow strips of fertile land lie along rivers traversing the coastal desert of Peru.

The late William Duncan Strong, while digging in 1946 in the Virú Valley, just south of the Moche Valley, unearthed a room that probably had been a Mochica tavern serving chicha. It contained four large pots similar to those used today for brewing the corn beer. The largest contained the mummified body of an old woman. Perhaps she had been the proprietress — the favorite village barmaid — buried by her devoted clients in the place where they best remembered her.

In the valley of the meandering Moche River a sweeping curve of desert nudges against green agricultural plots. On the sands, useless for farming, the Mochica through the centuries built temples honoring their gods. Masons toiled for years to construct the Huaca del Sol, or Temple of the Sun, laying an estimated 130 million adobe bricks. The structure covers eight acres, and the pyramid platform with its summit temple towers 135 feet above the desert floor. Near it stands the smaller Temple of the Moon. A fresco in one of its rooms, destroyed sometime after its discovery, was once bright with red, black, white, yellow, light blue, pink, and brown paints that depicted shields, maces, and darts with tiny arms and legs engaged in battle with humans. The animated weapons appeared to have the advantage over their foes.

Mochica engineering feats etch the desert between the Moche and Chicama Valleys. La Cumbre Canal, reaching 75 miles along the Chicama River, is still in use today. Aqueducts spanned ravines in the hills. One, built 50 feet high, stretches nearly a mile. Sections of Mochica roads remain visible today.

What for me is the most fascinating single burial yet found in Peru came to light during William Duncan Strong's expedition. Beginning one day at dawn and digging deep, their faces plastered with desert dust, the excavators found the skeleton of a powerfully built man wrapped in fine cloth, his knees and ankles tightly bound. Offerings of food and pottery accompanied him. After hours of careful cleaning and recording, they removed the skeleton and found just beneath it a cane sarcophagus with a headless llama on top. Another decapitated llama and two women, also sacrificed, lay close against the casket.

It was late afternoon. From miles away the Andes blew cold whispers against the men's backs deep within the shadowed pit. Slowly they opened the cane casket. Within lay offerings of pottery, feather headdresses, wooden batons, and a copper-shod staff topped with a wooden carving of the principal Mochica deity, his fangs of white shell glistening and his red painted eyes glaring beneath a jaguar headdress. The carved figure of a boy with a basket slung across his shoulder sowed seeds of turquoise as the god made furrows with a digging stick. Not until the offerings were cleared away and the archeologists began to investigate the bodies within did they realize what an astonishing find lay at their feet.

Under the offerings, in an unmistakable duplication of the carved figures, they found the remains of a warrior-priest personifying the god. His headdress of feathers and gilded copper bore a fanged animal at the front. On lifting the copper mask that covered his face the excavators saw that he was at death an aged, toothless man. His skin was as pallid and brittle as old parchment. Beside him were the remains of a boy of ten or twelve, with a rotting basket and bits of turquoise carved like kernels of corn. A war mace with the old priest showed the dents and scrapes of battle. Two Mochica warriors chased three smaller enemies in wooden pursuit around it. A battered eagle, outspread wings broken, perched on top.

The old warrior perhaps embodied the Mochica temperament for war. In any event militarism from another source would soon spell the doom of the Mochicas and their Nazca contemporaries. After A.D. 600, the history of Peru and the adjoining area to the south becomes, for the first time, one of empire, and two peoples play a part in the drama. One was centered just across the Peruvian border at Tiahuanaco in the Bolivian Andes not far from Lake Titicaca, the other at the city of Huari in Peru's southern highlands.

Tiahuanaco lies some 40 miles from La Paz, Bolivia's capital, in a bleak flatland so lofty it is always bathed in cold, a place where clouds ride columns of rain across stone ruins and the pottery-littered plain, and sometimes envelop the barren wastes in soft white mist.

Roughly hewn stones stand in nearby basalt and sandstone quarries; many remain where they were dragged into place but never incorporated into the buildings. Some stones in rows indicate the locations of buildings; others lie strewn about by the ravages of time and looters. Surrounding a core area lie nearly two square miles of ruins.

"The rumor that great abundance of riches was buried in these buildings," noted the Jesuit historian Bernabé Cobo in 1653, "has induced some Spaniards to excavate them in search of it and they have found at various times many pieces of gold and silver, though not as much as was thought to be there. . . . They have also despoiled it in order to make use of the stones. For the church of Tiahuanaco was built from them and the inhabitants of the town of Chuquiago (La Paz) carried off many to build their houses, and even the Indians in the village of Tiahuanaco make their tombs from beautiful stone tiles which they obtain from the ruins. . . ."

One architectural masterwork the looters left was the stone doorway, called the "Gateway of the Sun." Now re-erected, it stands alone, attached to nothing—wrought from a single piece of stone. On its upper facade a figure dubbed the "gateway god" stares straight ahead in bold relief, holding two staffs outward on either side. Covering the rest of the stone are 48 intricately carved winged figures frozen in a dead run facing toward the central god.

I N 1932 the late Wendell C. Bennett dug test pits at Tiahuanaco, unearthing the largest of the great human statues for which it is famed. Carved from a single block of red sandstone, the forbidding figure measures 24 feet in height. All the sculptures stand erect, forearms tight against their chests, eyes staring from squared heads, some topped with block helmets.

Tiahuanaco was apparently short-lived but highly influential, since pottery found from adjacent areas of Peru and all the way to Chile's Atacama Desert, 400 miles to the south, bears the same deities and follows the same rigid style. If Tiahuanaco was indeed the seat of its own southern empire, it also played a key role in the formation of another, some 400 miles to the north, whose center lay at the ancient highland city of Huari, near present-day Ayacucho.

"A strong relationship between Tiahuanaco and Huari is quite clear in their art," Alan Sawyer told us. "Designs on Huari textiles and pottery are remarkably similar to those on the Tiahuanaco monuments— even repeating the gateway god and the winged running 'messengers.' I think it's likely that the designs—the symbols of the religion of Tiahuanaco—were brought to Huari through the medium of textiles."

Renowned city of the Incas, Machu Picchu crowds a mountain ridge near Cuzco, Peru. This detailed section of a drawing published in 1930 reveals the heart of the complex. Stairway of the Fountains, named for nearby water basins and conduits, rises in the right foreground. To the left of the stair, in the center of the Royal Mausoleum Group, stands a semicircular temple, anchored to a crag by hewn stone blocks fitted to the ledge. Imperial residences lie to the right; agricultural terraces cover the slope at far left.

The Huari movement swept most Peruvian cultures, including those of the Mochicas and the Nazcas, into its empire. The archeological evidence is clear. "Everywhere in the stratigraphy," Gordon R. Willey of Harvard's Peabody Museum told me, "there is a continuation of common household pottery, but not of the highly decorated 'special pieces.' In the Moche area, for example, there is a complete cessation of the Mochica military themes so common earlier."

By A.D. 1000, times had changed again in ancient Peru. The Huari influence had waned, and small warring kingdoms and states began to rise in coastal valleys and in the highlands to fill the power vacuum.

Around the city of Trujillo, founded by Pizarro himself on the coast 300 miles northwest of present-day Lima, the cold ocean current often tantalizes the desert with gray, oppressive fog; when it lifts, the coast is as dry and barren as before. Trujillo lies at the mouth of the Moche River, only a few miles from the adobe brick temple, the Huaca del Sol, that commemorates the Mochica habitation of the valley. Just outside Trujillo to the northwest sprawl the remains of Chan Chan, seat of the Chimú kingdom between the 11th and 15th centuries, and the largest city ever built in ancient Peru.

The ruins of the great adobe city, though reduced by the encroachment of modern agriculture, still cover some nine square miles. Viewed from the air, the patterns are defined by a grid of eroded walls contained in nine gigantic rectilinear compounds whose walls—sometimes as many as three, running parallel—dominate the overall pattern. Within lie temple clusters, houses, and the dark rectangles of ancient marsh-clogged walk-in wells. Between the compounds runs the faint tracery of other smaller structures and cemeteries.

In clearing away the debris that erodes from the top of Chan Chan's walls, archeologists have exposed traces of paint and relief designs that once adorned the surfaces. Molding the wet adobe, artisans of the city produced complex arabesques and bands of repeating birds, fish, fantastic animals, scrolls, and step motifs, many of which remind me of textile designs. After exposure, the adobe reliefs remain much as they looked 800 years ago until rainstorms—which usually occur no more than once or twice a century—melt them away.

Archeologists Michael E. Moseley and Carol J. Mackey, excavating at Chan Chan with National Geographic Society aid, speculate that the compounds—one covers 45 acres—served the city's rulers as palaces, treasuries, and, finally, mausoleums. Most of the general populace lived in small quarters crowded against one edge of the great system of royal precincts. By estimating the number of such dwellings they have extrapolated Chan Chan's peak population at some 50,000.

With the urbanization so apparent at Chan Chan came mass production. I was particularly intrigued by the fact that most Chimú pottery, often quickly cast in molds, is of poorer quality than that of the earlier Mochicas. The few graves left untouched by Spanish treasure hunters and later huaqueros bespeak the wide separation between the social classes.

"Some of these are simple, with few and poor gifts," noted the late J. Alden Mason of the University of Pennsylvania, "while others consist of large subterranean chambers with quantities of pottery vessels, textiles, ornaments, and similar grave furniture."

Cat-faced god, 21 inches high, snarls from a plaque found at Chavín de Huantar, Peru. The Chavín style, inspired by a pervasive religious cult, spread across much of Peru beginning about 900 B.C. and endured for some five centuries. Intricate Chavín designs transform hair into snakes; jaguar mouths on both animal and human figures possibly denote super-natural power.

RICHARD SCHLECHT, AFTER MILTON F. SONDAY, JR., IN ALAN R. SAWYER, "ANCIENT PERUVIAN CERAMICS: THE NATHAN CUMMINGS COLLECTION," 1966

From later Inca accounts of the Chimú kingdom, recorded by the Spanish, I learned some of the names and dates of its century of glory. Around A.D. 1370 King Ñançen-pinco began the conquest of neighboring coastal peoples. Successive rulers continued the expansion over the next century until the Chimú controlled territory as far as the Lambayeque Valley to the north and the Casma Valley to the south—a coastal span of some 200 miles.

The high adobe walls of Chan Chan must have seemed impenetrable in the late 1400's when the Inca armies swept out of the highlands. But the invaders, undeterred, conquered the city with an ironically simple tactic. They diverted the canals, cutting off the city's water supply. Thus the largest of Peru's coastal kingdoms became subject to the land's last ancient empire.

Many of Cuzco's streets bear mute traces of those days when it was the royal city of the Incas. In narrow cobbled alleyways, walls of irregular unmortared masonry, finely cut and smoothed, and still—despite many earthquakes—tightly fitted, support the colonial and modern buildings that have long since replaced the upper structures. Even larger fitted megaliths comprise the huge fortress of Sacsahuaman. Its three parallel ramparts zigzag across the outer face of the hill that rises above Cuzco.

Suspended from masonry piers on cables of twigs and vines, an Inca bridge spans a gorge in the Andes. Incas united their domains with a road network that sped relay runners throughout the empire.

RICHARD SCHLECHT

S PANISH CHRONICLERS recorded in detail much of the story of the Incas—their customs, religion, language, government, and their triumphs and tragedies. The great Inca Empire had its beginnings in the Valley of Cuzco when a people calling themselves "the Children of the Sun" defeated their neighboring enemies, the Chancas, who had attacked Cuzco in the 1430's. Pachacuti Inca Yupanqui, commander of the Cuzco troops, became Inca, or ruler. Under his powerful direction, and that of two successors, Topa Inca Yupanqui and Huayna Capac, the empire rose to its full power in the 1480's, embracing all of western South America from the northern border of present-day Ecuador to the Maule River at Chile's midpoint.

For the Incas, conquest was largely a matter of diplomacy backed by military might. Troops would arrive in force at the borders of a desirable valley or kingdom; then envoys would cross and tell the local leader that he could remain in charge, but with curtailed power. Those who chose to resist were eliminated and replaced by a leader loyal to the Inca.

To stem the possibility of revolt, the Incas sometimes transplanted entire populations, placing dissident groups among loyal peoples and in turn shifting established friends of the empire into areas of potential trouble. To further unify the varied peoples and languages that made a patchwork quilt of the empire, Quechua, the old language of the Children of the Sun, became the official language of commerce throughout the realm.

For all their accomplishments in diplomacy and empire-building, the Incas never developed a system of writing, but their method of recording numbers on knotted strings of the *quipu*—unique in the New World—served almost as well.

The use of quipus may date from pre-Inca times, and in basic form the device survives even today in parts of Peru and Bolivia. It is one of varicolored string—cotton or wool—and consists of a principal cord with others of differing lengths attached, whose knots and the spacing between them record numbers of varying magnitude in a decimal system like that we use today. In the absence of written documents the quipu served the Incas as a memory device—specially trained keepers could read from the knotted strings such diverse details as population figures and the dates of historical events.

For the Inca Empire, just as for the similar empire of the Huari that preceded it, there is a wealth of evidence both for its spread and for the location of its capital. Ruins in Peru and beyond are built in the Cuzco style. Architecture along the coast employs the tight-fitting stone and adobe construction with the characteristic Inca trapezoidal wall niches. Pottery specimens, if not direct imports from Cuzco, are often imitations of the Cuzco wares, and bronze tools of Inca manufacture are found over the whole area. Thus, even without the records of the conquistadors, explained Alfred V. Kidder II of Philadelphia's University Museum, "it would have been possible to infer quite clearly the existence of an empire and to locate its capital at Cuzco."

SWIFT RUNNERS kept all parts of that empire in constant communication over the great system of coast and highland roads that still crisscross the land. Depending on the terrain, government messages and luxuries such as fresh fish traveled by runner a mile or two at a stretch. At rest houses along the way other couriers waited to snatch the packets or memorize the messages and speed them on. The Inca himself traveled in a litter plated with gold, and a thousand or more noblemen accompanied him as bearers. Noted a Spanish chronicler, "wherever he was expected to pass, the way was always scattered with sweet-smelling flowers and branches."

Every able-bodied adult of the realm worked, and every province paid tributes of gold, silver, llamas, food, or whatever the Inca determined it could afford. Orphans, the aged, and the sick of the empire received generous welfare grants from the government storehouses; vast supplies of corn, enough to feed the entire population in time of drought, were held in reserve.

Huayna Capac died in 1525, leaving his sons Huascar and Atahuallpa to split the empire in civil war that still raged when Pizarro reached the town of Cajamarca. Atahuallpa, who had captured and killed his brother, suffered the same fate at the hand of Pizarro. With that death the whole Inca world began to collapse.

European domination left its influence on Peru—just as had the Chavín cult, the Huari, and the Inca—and eventually extended to nearly all the native peoples of South America. As before, new cultures evolved from the blend. Peoples, never static after long contact with others, develop new ways and cling to old in a ratio that varies in ever-changing patterns across the loom of time.

Today many ancient patterns still survive in South America. An Amazon fisherman poises to spear his kill from a dugout; lowland manioc farmers tend their crops; tillers of Andean corn chew coca and drink chicha; and high in the misty mountains of Bolivia an Indian, like his ancestors, lashes together bundles of reeds for a boat, adds a woven-reed sail, and skims the chill blue waters of Lake Titicaca.

Irrigation channels wind through fields of fertile volcanic ash high in the Andes near Cajabamba, Ecuador. Pre-Columbian peoples of South America built extensive watering systems. Centralized governments ensured upkeep and fair distribution. Many ancient channels still function today.

LOREN McINTYRE

HUMBLEST DRAMA OF THE ANDES: THE TIMELESS TOIL FOR FOOD

"...the moon-shaped stone grinds whatever comes under it by its own weight and the Indian women can easily handle it because of its shape..." wrote Garcilaso de la Vega, son of a conquistador and an Inca princess, in 1609. In the Andes, Indian culinary methods have changed little in 350 years. Below, a derby-hatted Aymara woman of Peru grinds barley used in thickening soups and stews. Ancient South American peoples cultivated many staple crops such as corn, beans, and squash. The white potato originated in the Andes, but, for more than two centuries after the Spanish Conquest of Peru, Europe shunned the strange new plant, called *papa* by the Incas. They preserved potatoes by repeatedly squeezing out the water (above) and exposing them to sun and frost. *Chuño,* "potato dried on ice," provided nourishment on journeys. At left, an Aymara Indian of Bolivia stamps on *oca,* tubers closely related to potatoes, to hasten dehydration.

JOURNEY TO MACHU PICCHU, "LOST CITY OF THE INCAS"

"The road, following in large part an ancient footpath, is sometimes cut out of the side of sheer precipices, and at others is obliged to run on frail brackets propped against the side of overhanging cliffs," reported Hiram Bingham, leader of the 1912 National Geographic Society-Yale University Expedition to Machu Picchu. At right, the 11-man party rounds a bend near the ruins, above the swirling Urubamba River. The formidable journey to the city involved loading equipment onto a makeshift raft and coaxing pack animals across the Apurimac River in southern Peru (above). Bingham discovered Machu Picchu in 1911. After studying old chronicles, he determined that many Incas had fled there after being attacked and defeated by barbarians. If so, the Indians chose their place of refuge well. Machu Picchu, perched on the saddle between two mountains, lay "in the most inaccessible part of the Andes." Defended by natural bulwarks and concealed by foliage, the city escaped Spanish detection. After conquistadors killed the last emperor, Bingham theorized, the Incas abandoned the city. It remained lost to the outside world until he arrived centuries later.

GRANITE AND GOLD MASTERWORKS TESTIFY TO THE SKILL OF INDIAN ARTISANS

Vanished South American civilizations achieved astonishing mastery of architectural and metallurgical techniques. With stone hammers and bronze crowbars the Incas built the white-granite city of Machu Picchu (left). Rows of gabled houses extend from the Sacred Plaza; the Principal Temple stands at left, background; beyond the city, at right, towers Huayna, "Young," Picchu. The Inca wall in Cuzco (below) for centuries has withstood earthquakes that toppled Spanish-colonial and modern structures. By hammering out a hollow gold casting, a smith from the Tolima region of Colombia created the 5¼-inch-high stylized bird pendant more than 1,700 years ago. Knifelike bases of Tolima pendants suggest evolution from cutting implements. Experts in solid gold casting molded the 4-inch-high mace-bearing figurine in the Quimbaya style of Colombia's Cauca Valley at least 500 years ago. Quimbaya statuettes, distinguished by rounded contours and glistening surfaces, display "false filigree" like that of the fine bands on the ears and chest of this burnished figure.

N.G.S. PHOTOGRAPHER BATES LITTLEHALES (OPPOSITE AND BOTTOM) AND VICTOR R. BOSWELL, JR., AND JAMES E. RUSSELL, N.G.S. STAFF; MUSEUM OF THE AMERICAN INDIAN, HEYE FOUNDATION, NEW YORK (UPPER LEFT), AND COURTESY WILLIAM B. JAFFE (UPPER RIGHT)

GAZING ACROSS CENTURIES

Author Stuart examines mace heads of copper and polished stone—murderous skull-breakers when fitted with wooden hafts. Warriors of Peru wielded such weapons through two and a half millenniums. At right, stylized eyes stare from an effigy jar fashioned in the third century B.C. by an artisan of southern Peru's Ica Valley. Shoulders and hips bear masks of the deity of a trophy-head cult; a trophy head appears above a two-headed serpent. The ceramic arm at left, also of the Ica Valley, bears stylized cats and birds and a human figure in the palm. A powerful culture called the Tiahuanaco created the shell and turquoise inlaid mirror at far left around A.D. 1000. Polished iron pyrites served as the mirror's face.

ANCIENT AND MODERN TEXTILES OF PERU: 45 CENTURIES OF WOVEN ARTISTRY

Handwoven, multicolored fabrics like the poncho worn by the Peruvian Indian above exemplify the continuing glory of Andean civilization. Indians of Peru produced textiles as early as 2500 B.C., when they began to cultivate cotton. Skilled spinners and dyers, they obtained wool from the llama, alpaca, guanaco, and vicuña. The coastal-dwelling Paracas people employed diverse weaving techniques to create embroidery and lace-like gauze. The rich mantle detail below, embroidered on woven cloth to form a sea deity, decorated a mummy wrapping from a 2,000-year-old grave; the aridity of the Paracas Necropolis preserved it. Today, Peruvians perpetuate the tradition of splendid textiles on a treadle loom (right) such as the Spanish introduced.

CHAN CHAN, CITY OF KINGS Sun-baked remains of hundreds of rooms sprawl across the coastal desert of northern Peru. Beginning in the 13th century A.D. each of nine kings of the Chimú

DAVID BRILL

empire built such a royal compound to serve as palace, coffer, and crypt. Invaded by highland Incas in the late 15th century and plundered since the Spanish Con-

quest in the 1530's, Chan Chan faces modern threats: Squatters plow a third of the ruins; treasure seekers ransack burial platforms like the one at lower right.

SOUTH AMERICA OFFERS AN IMMENSE CHALLENGE TO ARCHEOLOGISTS

On this vast continent uncounted sites await exploration; many known ruins require years of further study. Locations range from coastal deserts to towering peaks. Archeological periods span hundreds of centuries, from primitive nomadism to complex urban life. Stone blades, scrapers, and projectile points (below) lie scattered in a Peruvian desert, untouched for 7,000 years. Around A.D. 1000 the powerful Chimú supplanted the Huari at Pacatnamú, now a buried ruin (right) on Peru's north coast. Archeologists have made only limited excavations at this site, continuously inhabited for 2,000 years before the Conquest. The Incas constructed the garrison at Ollantaytambo (above) of stone and adobe, an engineering triumph in the precipitous Andes.

7

ENDLESS SEARCH

Archeologists apply the newest tools of science and technology
in the quest for the secrets of American prehistory

THE BROAD OUTLINE of man's life and achievements in the Americas during the 12,000 years prior to the arrival of the Europeans is now known, but enough significant questions remain to challenge archeology and its methods for generations to come.

Those methods multiply and improve daily, affecting both the recovery of archeological material and its interpretation. Increasingly complex sensing devices locate hidden building foundations or massive sculptures; simple wooden boxes, shaken as if sluicing for gold, float out even the smallest seeds and vegetable remains that betray early plant life, diet, and climate. While radiocarbon and tree-ring dating methods are constantly refined, the dating of obsidian tools by measuring the extent of surface penetration of microscopic traces of absorbed moisture has come into practice. This technique gives us valuable cross-checks on dates gleaned by other methods.

In addition, new theoretical approaches attempt more exact and valid correlations between the artifact and the person who made it. In a grand assault by computer some archeologists have even analyzed the patterns of distribution of varying pottery decoration recovered from separate dwellings of a single site, and have suggested that the patterns reflect marriage customs—some in which the bride (assumed to be the potter) moved into the household of her husband's parents; others in which the husband moved to the wife's household.

Rising with the sun at Becan, archeologists climb a precipitous Maya
pyramid, one of thousands of unexcavated ruins in Mexico. The enigma of
the 9-inch-high Ecuadorian house model (above) also challenges scholars.
Its Oriental style suggests transpacific contact some 2,000 years ago.

So far the computer has proved highly effective in analyzing artifacts for variations that may reflect more than meets the eye. In a fraction of the time men would take, computers perform complex intercorrelations of such measurable characteristics of stone tools as length, thickness, shape, and angle of edge chipping. At Cahokia, Illinois, a skeleton entombed a thousand years lay with a huge cache of projectile points carefully arranged into types by the burial attendants. Can modern scientists recover to even a limited extent the subtleties that may have governed such placement of stone tools by a mind of another culture and another time? The Cahokia discovery gave archeologists the opportunity to test such a possibility. They fed random data on size and shape of the points into a computer, and it produced the same arrangement found in the cache.

Perhaps the archeologists' most fundamental problems surround the relationship between ancient cultures of the Americas and those of Europe and Asia. Gordon R. Willey of Harvard University's Peabody Museum characterizes these problems as "to a very large extent, what American archeology is about," and they include two of the most controversial subjects of New World prehistory—the date of man's first entry and the nature of transoceanic contact with the Old World before Columbus ushered in the Age of Discovery.

"If anthropology has taught us anything," Bob Humphrey said to me one day as we discussed the peopling of the Americas, "it is that human culture is unbelievably complex, so it's most unlikely that there are simple answers to questions dealing with perhaps 20,000 years of it over such a large area."

Considering the fragmentary nature of the archeological evidence of early man, and the luck involved in even finding the very oldest sites in any number, the problem is magnified to a tremendous degree.

Moving backward past the 10th millennium B.C. into the remote times before the Clovis hunter roamed North America, archeologists of both continents abruptly encounter fewer dates associated with human remains or artifacts. This leads some to consider 11,000 to 10,000 B.C. as the probable earliest time for man in the Americas. Others theorize that men may have come out of Asia as long ago as 40,000 years.

Kindred tripod vessels, the one above fashioned of bronze 2,000 years ago in China and the other of clay in Guatemala 400 years later, hint at transpacific contact. Some authorities believe that storm winds and ocean currents carried Oriental ships to the Americas, giving rise to cultural similarities.

I N THE LIGHT of present knowledge, however, the honored superlative "oldest" cannot be applied with complete confidence to anything much earlier than 10,000 B.C. No excavation has as yet unearthed any artifact directly underlying a Clovis stratum. But isolated finds do raise the distinct possibility of much earlier entry by man. Perhaps the oldest site now known will prove to be the lowest level at Wilson Butte Cave, Idaho, with stone tools dated by radiocarbon tests of related organic material at 12,550 B.C., plus or minus a possible error of 500 years; or the comparably dated material from Fort Rock Cave, Oregon; from El Jobo, Venezuela; or from Tagua Tagua, Chile. The earliest evidence may well go back *another* 10,000 years. At Tlapacoya, southeast of Mexico City, archeologists found an obsidian blade beneath the remains of a log dated at 21,200 B.C. Part of a human skull found nearby in 1969 may prove to be just as old. Still speculative are the chipped stones excavated in the mid-1960's at the Calico site about five miles northeast of Yermo, California. Some scientists think the roughly flaked

RICHARD SCHLECHT

stones are the work of man, and date from at least 40,000 B.C. Others are equally convinced that they are fortuitous products of nature. To the question of the oldest remains, then, there is only one possible answer at this stage of research: Consider all the evidence and make your choice.

Legends of sunken continents and early theories that all civilization came out of Egypt are now largely dispelled, but they long lent an air of the ridiculous to any contention that there may have been actual trans-oceanic contact between peoples of the Old World and those of the New before the time of Columbus. In the past decade, however, many archeologists have begun the objective appraisal of evidence that such contact, no matter how tenuous or accidental, did indeed take place across the Atlantic, with the Vikings, and possibly the Pacific.

On the Guayas coast of Ecuador, just north of the Gulf of Guayaquil, archeologists Betty J. Meggers, Clifford Evans, and the late Emilio Estrada in 1956 and 1957 found pottery fragments of a local phase of prehistory later labeled Valdivia. The date—around 2500 B.C.—puts it among the oldest pottery yet found in the Americas. Valdivia pottery appears suddenly in the stratigraphy of adjacent coastal sites. The ware that most closely resembles it lies some 9,500 miles across the Pacific, in Jomon Period sites of southern Kyushu, Japan.

"Words can't express adequately the degree of similarity between early Valdivia and contemporary Jomon pottery," Clifford Evans told me. "Many fragments of both are so similar in appearance that they might almost have come from the same vessel."

Both the Ecuadorian and the Japanese pottery include decorations with broad incised lines, vertical and horizontal zigzags, nested squares, and intricate patterns of cross-hatching. Some sherds bear identical patterns of punctation or wavy bands sketched on the wet clay with the serrate edge of a seashell.

Similarity between artifacts alone, of course, does not necessarily mean contact between two areas, but in this case coincidence seemed unusually vulnerable because of the remarkable correspondence of form and so many methods of decoration. Meggers, Evans, and Estrada carefully considered many other circumstances that bore on their find; all reinforced the possibility of direct influence from Japan to Ecuador. First, the chronological relationship: Early and Middle Jomon cultures appear roughly contemporary with Valdivia. Second, Japanese arche-ologists have recovered evidence of long and gradual evolution of pottery design and decoration in the Jomon sites; in Ecuador, on the other hand, the pottery appeared suddenly, fully developed, and without precedent. Third, the two cultures were strikingly sim-ilar, both consisting of fishing folk, increasing even further the prob-ability that the Valdivia people were "ready" for the innovation of pottery—in which they rapidly excelled their Japanese mentors in quality and artistry.

Was the long voyage from Japan physically possible? Yes, say the discoverers of Valdivia pottery, citing evidence of known boat types, ocean currents, and the ability of men, particularly fishermen, to sur-vive. If it did take place, they continue, "It can only be said with cer-tainty that the trip must have taken many months and that one or more members of the crew survived, probably well tanned!"

The possibility of a transpacific voyage in the third millennium B.C. has reopened a traditional and enduring argument among archeologists—the question of the diffusion of an idea versus its independent occurrence in separate areas. Transoceanic contact, some contend, explains parallels between the Old World and the New that range from the use of clay pottery and metallurgy to art styles and the appearance of such unusual artifacts as panpipes and miniature wheeled animal "toys." Others argue that such inventions could have taken place more than once, and did. Even granting occasional contact between the hemispheres, they deny the long-range effect of such contact on either the course or the character of New World culture.

The question touches equally on the relationship of remains within the Americas—the startlingly close duplication of architecture, pottery, and tools between the southwestern United States and the arid mesa country of northwestern Argentina; or the yet-unexplained and sudden appearance of Woodland pottery in the eastern United States in the first millenniums B.C. Such riddles abound, and today archeologists seek answers to them, and to others that pertain to cultural processes and chronologies in particular areas.

Beside the Kanawha River near St. Albans, West Virginia, Bettye J. Broyles of the West Virginia Geological and Economic Survey has spent several summers excavating a site that may turn out to be not only one of the oldest known in the eastern United States, but also one of the deepest ever excavated there.

"We know from six drill-core samples," Bettye told me, "that the St. Albans site contains almost 37 feet of successive occupation layers neatly separated by sterile river flood deposits, and this doesn't count the six feet of late deposits that were removed for highway fill in 1963."

So far, excavation has revealed 18 feet of layered prehistory at St. Albans, reaching from around 6000 B.C. back to about 8000 B.C. and showing a clear sequence of projectile-point types. Many are identical to those found in widely separated parts of the East, from Russell Cave, Alabama, to the Modoc Rock Shelter in Illinois, and to sites in Missouri. One flint point, found on the riverbank, resembles North Carolina's sometimes-fluted Hardaway points, possible successors to Paleo-Indian fluted points of the 10th millennium B.C.

"We have 10 charcoal samples being dated in the lab now," Bettye continued. "One came from a hearth 21 feet below the present surface. This date could turn out to be as early as 9000 B.C."

If it does, the 16 feet remaining beneath that hearth should extend well into the time of Paleo-Indian hunters and give archeologists a clear yardstick for measuring the life of early man in the eastern United States, the progress of his stone technology, and any climatic changes that might have taken place over the long span.

Half a hemisphere away—in Peru—archeologist Richard S. Mac-Neish has focused his attention on the Ayacucho Basin as a promising locale in which to document the origins of agriculture and trace the development of civilization in the central Andes. His excavations in the highland valley have produced unexpected bonuses: Deep in Pikima-chay Cave among the remains of Ice Age animals, he found rude choppers, scrapers, and other stone tools; one sloth bone sealed in the same deposit has been tentatively dated at 17,650 B.C.

An opportunity for me and my son George to participate in an excavation came during our family travels when E. Wyllys Andrews IV began research in the southeastern part of Mexico's Campeche State, under the sponsorship of the National Geographic Society and Tulane University. I had taken part in Bill Andrews's Dzibilchaltún dig in northern Yucatán from 1958 through 1960, and I was delighted when he asked if we would visit his new excavation.

The field camp lies at Xpuhil, almost at the precise center of the Yucatán Peninsula. The five thatched huts and screened laboratory were dark when George and I arrived one night about ten o'clock. Sensible bedtime for the next day's early rising had come and gone, but Bill and his lab assistant Eduardo Toro, awakened by the noise and lights of our jeep, greeted us. After a brief reunion they showed us to a hut where, in true Yucatecan fashion, we hung our hammocks.

L ATER, as I lay listening to a disconcerting rustle in the thatch directly overhead, I reflected on the place to which we had come. The rain forest stretches unbroken from Xpuhil to Tikal, 90 miles to the south, and beyond; north it extends a roughly equal distance to where towns begin to dot the arid northern landscape. On either side of Xpuhil for some 50 miles — except for a nearby lumber camp, some small settlements, and an airstrip — the area is as blank on maps as it is desolate in reality. Yet its forest hides remarkable concentrations of Maya ruins and unusually well-preserved temples.

I recalled that Karl Ruppert and John H. Denison, Jr., of the Carnegie Institution of Washington surveyed this area in the 1930's, mapping some 30 ruins. Two of the largest, Xpuhil and Becan, are very near the camp. Others, like Calakmul, lie to the south. Large, well-preserved pyramid-temples of Río Bec, which they cleared and charted, have become lost again — hidden by forest growth. Fatigue at last overcame the excitement of anticipation, and I slept deeply until a light shone through the screen door and a voice said, "It's four-thirty."

Soon George and I met the other members of Bill's 1969 expedition: graduate students Newell O. Wright, Jr., and Prentice M. Thomas of Tulane University; Michael Simmons and his wife Ellen, University of Arizona; and Jack D. Eaton, who had supervised construction of the field camp and explored much of the surrounding area. After breakfast we loaded canteens, notebooks, and lunches into trucks and left camp for the ruins of Becan just as sunrise burnished the morning mist.

"Our excavations," Bill explained as we rode, "are concentrated on Becan this season, then we'll move on to other sites nearby. We're in an area that culturally, as well as geographically, lies between northern Yucatán and the Petén area of Guatemala's panhandle, and their archeological similarities and differences overlap here.

"Some of the ruins," Bill continued, "closely resemble those at Tikal and the other Petén centers; others, by virtue of their architectural style and lack of hieroglyphic inscriptions, are related to sites in the north — Uxmal and others in the Puuc area, and the similar Maya buildings at Chichén Itzá. The big question is whether the Late Classic sites like Tikal were contemporary with the northern centers, or earlier, as our excavations at Dzibilchaltún suggested. Trying to correlate stratigraphy between the two areas has not shed much light on the problem.

"The answer should lie here," he finished, gesturing out the window.

We had gone nearly four miles east, when Bill pointed toward what seemed to be a large forested island rising from the plain to the right of the road. Becan.

"Already, we've gained an unexpected bonus from our test pits here," he remarked. "The earliest pottery goes all the way back to about 500 B.C., and the latest into the centuries just before the Spanish Conquest. That's quite a span of occupation, and we really didn't expect to be so lucky in our very first excavations."

On the map drawn by Ruppert and Denison, Becan consists of four main connected plazas, raised some 30 feet above the plain and each bordered by large pyramid-temples. A moat, crossed here and there by causeways, surrounds this heart of the site.

"The place must have presented quite a view from a distance," Bill said as we parked in a clearing beside the moat. "The backs of the major pyramids, from ground level to summits, apparently consisted of stepped tiers of vaulted rooms that faced outward, away from the raised interior plazas."

We filed up the slope onto the first plaza. The sun had by then dispersed the mist; the morning had grown hotter; and the light played over the huge heaps of stone and their dense cover of tall trees. Here and there I could pick out the regularity of a partially exposed vault, a shifted stairway, or clean vertical walls and sharp corners of smooth gray stone that showed the immensity of the summit temples.

Prentice Thomas and a few workmen, carrying shovels, trowels, and a propane lamp, began climbing the steep rubble slope of the largest structure facing the plaza. Their task for the day: to continue the excavation of one of the intact inner chambers behind and slightly below the summit temple, seeking pottery samples from the dusty fill. Newell Wright departed by another trail to continue his excavation of a tiny platform on the flat ground behind the plaza. George, Bill, and I walked across the rock-strewn plaza and headed for the ball court, some distance away.

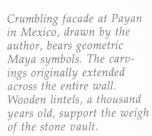

Crumbling facade at Payan in Mexico, drawn by the author, bears geometric Maya symbols. The carvings originally extended across the entire wall. Wooden lintels, a thousand years old, support the weigh of the stone vault.

GEORGE E. STUART, N.G.S. STAFF

T HE TRAIL wound through bush hung with lianas and occasionally draped with clumps of orchids, up the rocky edges of platforms and over rubble mounds. At one point we skirted a partially standing vault that made a long black tunnel in the slope. In the second plaza rose a featureless heap of stone larger than the Castillo at Chichén Itzá. Near it, a carved stela, eroded into shapeless lumps, was gripped firmly by the tree roots that had broken it. We passed another huge pile, with parts of an ornamental facade still in place beside the dark doorway of its temple, then another smaller ruin, and arrived at the parallel mounds that mark the ball court.

"We've cleared away most of the rubble," Bill pointed out, "so the ball court is ready to be measured and drawn. As yet we haven't found any ball rings, if indeed there are any here."

While my son George measured and called out the figures to me, I transferred them onto a scaled diagram, then sketched details of the masonry. The size of the stones and the character of their finish and shape are often useful in differentiating between various stages of building within a structure. We finished our task in about an hour,

made the hot walk back to the first plaza for lunch, then returned to the lab, where Ellen and Eduardo were numbering the thousands of pottery fragments that covered the tables—all brought in from test pits and excavations at Becan. By four o'clock the rest of the crew had returned from the site for showers, supper, and a short time of relaxation.

Subsequent days passed much like the first. I made drawings of a small round platform, more pottery sherds, and the position of a cache of nine flint blades in Newell Wright's small platform. Bill took us to two more sites near Xpuhil—the damaged temple of Payan, and the nearly intact building that Jack Eaton had discovered deep in the bush across the road from Becan. Realizing that each day might well bring further discoveries, perhaps a glyph-covered monument or even a whole new site, we regretfully left for Mérida.

There's a great deal of satisfaction in transferring archeological finds to paper; such sketches form the basis for the interpretation of the data, ranging from stone tools to temples, that time has distilled from an incredibly complex human past and bequeathed to the present.

To gain insight into the mentalities and motivations of the people who acted out that long drama, the archeologist, who is after all first an anthropologist, must often resort to a methodical comparison of living peoples and their artifacts with the material remains of the past. By such careful analogy shadowy vignettes begin to take shape, and one can attempt to visualize a Maya priest at Tikal or Becan teaching novices the meaning of the hieroglyphs; a ball game at the great Hohokam court in Snaketown, Arizona; the burial ceremonies that must have accompanied the interments of the Etowah priest-chiefs in their log tombs in Mound C; or a Paracas master weaver at work two millenniums ago in southern Peru.

Many details—too many—can never be known: The archeologist

instinctively wishes to know more about the Southern Cult child buried at Etowah with a miniature copper plate and water bottle. By extension, since man is uniquely interested in his own kind, he wishes to know more of other individuals both great and ordinary who, with their sufferings and joys, their failures and achievements, helped weave the intricate tapestry of ancient American life.

The archeologist must work in simple dwelling mounds as well as in imposing temples; he must label sites and whole peoples as their remains come to light, and by thorough and painstaking cross-comparison assign them positions on time-period charts and on tables of recognizable cultural traditions compiled during years of research. From all this, the general sweep of American prehistory has begun to take shape as a living past, and, as time goes on, major revisions of the charts and tables should become fewer and fewer; minor changes will doubtless come as often as new data are incorporated and new areas explored in detail for the first time.

But every day more of the material of archeology is disappearing into the maw of modern civilization. The famous Olmec site of La Venta lies above an oil field; an airstrip bisects its ceremonial center; and at night flares of burning natural gas cast eerie shadows over the surrounding swamps and their iridescent scum. Oil, too, might spell the archeological doom of much of Alaska's Arctic slope, where lie ancient campsites so crucial to the understanding of man's entry into the Americas; underground nuclear testing in the Aleutian Islands has made many sites there inaccessible to the archeologist. The environs of Lima slowly spread outward over remains that mirror the history of Peru from pre-Chavín times to the Inca Empire. Other sites all over the United States and Latin America vanish beneath reservoirs, are bulldozed into oblivion by highway construction, or destroyed by collectors and seekers of salable treasure. Others are simply being eroded away by the processes of nature.

ONE DAY I picked up a copy of *American Antiquity*, the quarterly journal of the Society for American Archaeology, and turned to the current-research section that appears in the back of each issue. In it I counted more than 150 excavations carried out the previous summer in the United States alone, by universities, government agencies, and state archeological societies—a grand assault on sites that range from shell middens in Maine to a Paleo-Indian camp at Mockingbird Gap, New Mexico, where fluted Clovis points lie in the sand beside the debris of modern rocketry—framing a 12,000-year history of man's weaponry. With an intensity that matches the variety of their projects, archeologists pursue research over much of the hemisphere. And from the Bering Strait to Cape Horn, from Oregon to Florida, from the dry coast of Peru to the mouth of the Amazon, hundreds of thousands of undiscovered sites wait silently to tell their part in the story of man's past in the Americas.

Perhaps the mood of the scholars who seek those secrets is best expressed in the reply that Mexican archeologist César Saenz gave one day at Uxmal when Gregg asked him what he considered the greatest discovery he had ever made.

"That's easy," he replied. "It's always my latest."

From the bottom of a pit dug in a small rubble-filled platform at Becan, graduate student Newell O. Wright, Jr., hands up two of nine flint points found in a cache. Mexican workmen peer down from the surface. Archeologists visited the ruins of Becan as early as 1934; concentrated work began 35 years later.

UNEARTHING A JUMBLED PUZZLE OF PREHISTORY IN GUATEMALA

An unnamed culture at Monte Alto in southern Guatemala presents new questions to archeologists probing the origins and influence of the Olmecs. A team headed by Lee A. Parsons of the Peabody Museum, Harvard University, and supported by the National Geographic Society, began excavating the site late in 1968 and soon unearthed five massive sculptures like the rotund effigy opposite. Closed eyes may indicate death or sleep. Team members in the background measure a platform of rubble for a plan drawing. Five stone heads excavated here resemble the colossal heads of the Olmecs, perhaps representing very early Olmec or,

more likely, a provincial variation. Below, workmen carefully brush away dirt from a pottery cache. A greenstone mask (also shown above) rests in one of the two shallow bowls that held it. Since the mask predates the bowls by hundreds of years, Parsons speculates that later occupants of the site unearthed it and, regarding it as an heirloom, placed it between the protective bowls for reburial. The mask, perforated at eyes, ears, and nose, may have served as a face covering for the dead. The wife of one of the archeologists at Monte Alto works full time numbering and typing record cards for the thousands of potsherds found thus far.

MAGNETIC IMPULSES PIERCE THE EARTH AND PLOT THE POSITIONS OF BURIED ARTIFACTS

On the flank of an earthen pyramid at La Venta in Mexico archeologists hunt hidden sculptures of basalt, using a cesium magnetometer to detect the iron-rich stone. The searcher above, steadied by a line to the 100-foot-high summit, carries one of two sensors, probing continuously along his path; the second sensor, in a fixed position nearby, records the unwavering line of the earth's magnetic field. Seated before the magnetometer's read-out panel (below), a colleague charts variations in the signals that betray the presence of any object with a higher iron content than the sand and clay of the mound. Some 2,700 years ago the Olmecs began to raise this volcano-shaped pyramid. Robert F. Heizer of the University of California, working with the support of the National Geographic Society, theorizes that the Olmecs built the fluted cone to remind them of the smoldering peaks of their homeland, perhaps in the Tuxtla Mountains to the northwest.

AIRBORNE CAMERAS AID ARCHEOLOGISTS IN THE NORTH AMERICAN SUBARCTIC

Great Whale River on the east coast of Canada's Hudson Bay flows beneath the cameras of archeologist Elmer Harp, Jr., of Dartmouth College. The outskirts of Poste de la Baleine appear on the north shore in the natural-color photograph above. Identical scale permits size comparison with the camouflage-detection photograph below. In 1966, using several film types, Harp found about 30 tepee rings, each 12 to 15 feet across, that appear in both photographs as minute dots in the clearing on the south shore. Camouflage-detection film intrigues archeologists because it penetrates shadows and upsets the eye's color expectations.

ITEK CORPORATION, LEXINGTON, MASSACHUSETTS (OPPOSITE, ABOVE) AND RICHARD SCHLECHT (OPPOSITE BELOW)

IN GLEAMING LABORATORIES SCIENCE SPEEDS THE WORK OF ARCHEOLOGY

In the laboratory at the University Museum in Philadelphia, Mark C. Han (above) seeks to date pottery sherds by thermoluminescence, an experimental radiochemical technique. Its goal: to interpret the intensity of light that ceramics emit when sufficiently reheated and to correlate the results with the time elapsed since the clay's original firing. Below, Edwin N. Wilmsen of the University of Michigan studies a stone tool from the Lindenmeier site in Colorado (detail below left). He looks for microscopic edge scratches that suggest degree of use. Wilmsen has classified 20,000 Lindenmeier artifacts, preparing a computer card for each. He hopes the computer will help define the relationships of bands that stopped at the site over several generations.

NATIONAL GEOGRAPHIC PHOTOGRAPHER JAMES L. AMOS (ABOVE) AND LOWELL J. GEORGIA

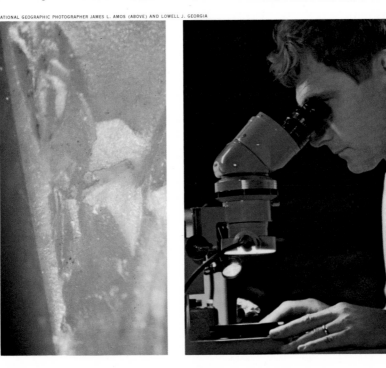

INFRARED PHOTOGRAPH DETECTS THE FAINT IMPRINT OF PREHISTORIC MAN

South Dakota farmland brightens to bizarre shades on infrared film: trees and other vegetation look bloodied and the Missouri River flows an inky blue-black (lower left); a plowed field appears pale green. Farmers have cultivated the field and planted it every spring since 1921, but it still bears the mark of an ancient settlement. The pattern shows clearly on infrared film, an experimental tool of aerial photography that archeologists have used in seeking prehistoric sites. The drawing below clarifies the photograph: traces of bastions surround small rings, possibly remnants of dwelling places, storage heaps, or refuse dumps. The larger, double circles mark locations of long-vanished Indian earth lodges. Though the Smithsonian Institution has made preliminary surveys and tests at the site, it still awaits careful excavation—like uncounted others throughout North and South America. Archeologists studying aerial photographs examine both the natural and cultural landscapes, looking for visible evidence—cleared fields, trails, earthworks—that man has occupied a site. Traces of his habitation often remain at what archeologists call the "threshold of recognition," invisible from the ground but, like the defensive earthworks above, startlingly clear from the air.

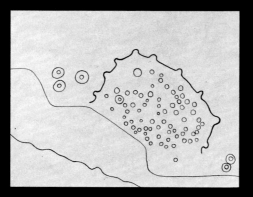

ALAN R. SAWYER (ABOVE) AND PEDRO ROJAS PONCE

REMOTE PERUVIAN SITES WAIT TO TELL THEIR STORIES

Pockmarked by craters left by *huaqueros,* or treasure hunters, an unnamed site sprawls across a desert ridge in Peru. Invisible from the valleys on either side, the deeply eroded plateau nestles between the converging Palpa River and the Río Grande de Nazca near the country's southern coast. Stonework friezes in the two pictures at left ornament the exterior walls of round temple platforms at Pajatén, a site on the jungle-cloaked eastern slopes of the Andes in northern Peru. At far left, a condor spreads wings of stone. On another frieze, seated human figures wear feather crowns. The rugged terrain of the area has placed these ruins beyond the reach of huaqueros; many such sites lie in dense tropical vegetation, awaiting the attention of the archeologist.

205

ARCHEOLOGICAL SECRETS LIE HIDDEN IN THE MISTS OF A MEXICAN JUNGLE

In a stairwell infested with bats and cockroaches, archeologists explore a rock-walled tunnel within a pyramid at Becan. Below, author Stuart draws a Maya facade at nearby Payan (finished drawing pages 194-95) as E. Wyllys Andrews calls out measurements. At its height, Becan consisted of four main plazas rimmed by pyramid-temples. Rooms within the structures, per-

haps occupied by priests, faced outward and away from the plazas. Graduate students (opposite) investigate the crumbling ruin; a doorway lures one of them. Working painstakingly at sites like this, 20th-century archeologists sift the rubble of millenniums for clues to the lives of early Americans, but time obscures the unchronicled past as surely as mist shrouds the jungle.

INDEX

Illustrations references appear in italics

Guide to Pronunciation

Cajamarca — kah-hah-MAR-kah
Chapultepec — cha-POOL-teh-pek
Dzibilchaltún — dzee-beel-chahl-TOON
El Tajín — el tah-HEEN
Huaca Prieta — wah-kah pree-AY-tah
Kaminaljuyú — kah-mee-nahl-hoo-YOO
Mixtec — MEESH-tek
Oaxaca — wah-HAH-kah
Quetzalcóatl — ket-sahl-COH-ahtl

Sacsahuaman — sahk-sah-wah-MAHN
Tenochtitlán — teh-noch-teet-LAHN
Teotihuacán — tay-oh-tee-wah-KAHN
Tepexpan — teh-pesh-PAHN
Texcoco — tehs-KOH-koh
Tezcatlipóca — tehs-kah-tlee-POH-kah
Tiahuanáco — tee-ah-wah-NAH-koh
Uxmal — oosh-MAHL
Xpuhil — shpoo-HEEL

Additional References

For additional reading, you may wish to refer to the following books and NATIONAL GEOGRAPHIC articles and to check the Society's Cumulative Index for related material: E. Wyllys Andrews, IV, "Dzibilchaltun: Lost City of the Maya," Jan. 1959; Alfonso Caso, "Monte Albán, Richest Archeological Find in America," Oct. 1932; Henry B. Collins, "Vanished Mystery Men of Hudson Bay," Nov. 1956; Eusebio Dávalos Hurtado, "Into the Well of Sacrifice—I" (Chichén Itzá), Oct. 1961; Emil W. Haury, "The Hohokam: First Masters of the American Desert," May 1967.

Helge Ingstad, "Vinland Ruins Prove Vikings Found the New World," Nov. 1964; Neil M. Judd, "Everyday Life in Pueblo Bonito," Sept. 1925; Bates Littlehales, "Into the Well of Sacrifice—II" (Chichén Itzá), Oct. 1961; Bart McDowell, "Mexico's Window on the Past," Oct. 1968; Loren McIntyre, "The Lost Empire of the Incas," Dec. 1973; Michael E. Moseley and Carol J. Mackey, "Chan Chan, Peru's Ancient City of Kings," March 1973; Froelich G. Rainey, "Discovering Alaska's Oldest Arctic Town" (Ipiutak), Sept. 1942.

Matthew W. Stirling, "Discovering the New World's Oldest Dated Work of Man," Aug. 1939; "Expedition Unearths Buried Masterpieces of Carved Jade" (Cerro de las Mesas, Mexico), Sept. 1941; "Hunting Prehistory in Panama Jungles," Aug. 1953; "La Venta's Green Stone Tigers" (Mexico), Sept. 1943; and "On the Trail of La Venta Man" (Mexico), Feb. 1947; Matthew W. and Marion Stirling, "Finding Jewels of Jade in a Mexican Swamp" (La Venta), Nov. 1942; William Duncan Strong, "Finding the Tomb of a Warrior-God," Apr. 1947; George E. Stuart, "Who Were the 'Mound Builders'?," Dec. 1972; Herman von Walde-Waldegg, "Stone Idols of the Andes Reveal a Vanished People," May 1940; Kenneth F. Weaver, "Magnetic Clues Help Date the Past," May 1967.

CHAPTER 1: Garcilaso de la Vega, *The Florida of the Inca,* John Grier Varner and Jeannette Johnson Varner, translators, 1951; Bernal Díaz del Castillo, *The Discovery and Conquest of Mexico,* 1956; Augustín de Zárate, *The Discovery and Conquest of Peru,* J. M. Cohen, translator, 1968.

CHAPTER 2: Richard S. MacNeish, "The Origins of New World Civilization," *Scientific American,* Nov. 1964; H. M. Wormington, *Ancient Man in North America,* 1957.

CHAPTER 3: Ignacio Bernal, *Mexico before Cortez: Art, History, Legend,* 1963; Michael D. Coe, *America's First Civilization,* 1968; George E. Stuart, National Geographic Society Archeological Map of Middle America, 1968; J. Eric S. Thompson, *The Rise and Fall of Maya Civilization,* 1966.

CHAPTER 4: Alfred V. Kidder, *An Introduction to the Study of Southwestern Archaeology,* 1962; Clyde Kluckhohn and Dorothea Leighton, *The Navaho,* 1962; Paul S. Martin, *Digging into History,* 1959; Don Watson, *Indians of the Mesa Verde,* 1955.

CHAPTER 5: Emma Lila Fundaburk and Mary Douglass Fundaburk Foreman, *Sun Circles and Human Hands,* 1957; T. M. N. Lewis and Madeline Kneberg, *Tribes that Slumber,* 1958; Robert Silverberg, *Mound Builders of Ancient America,* 1968.

CHAPTER 6: Edward P. Lanning, *Peru Before the Incas,* 1967; J. Alden Mason, *The Ancient Civilizations of Peru,* 1968; G. Reichel-Dolmatoff, *Colombia,* 1965; Alan R. Sawyer, *Mastercraftsmen of Ancient Peru,* 1968.

CHAPTER 7: Kwang Chih Chang, *Rethinking Archaeology,* 1967; James Deetz, *Invitation to Archaeology,* 1967; Betty J. Meggers, *Ecuador,* 1966.

GENERAL: Jesse D. Jennings and Edward Norbeck, editors, *Prehistoric Man in the New World,* 1964; Charles R. McGimsey III, *Public Archeology,* 1972; John Howland Rowe, "Archaeology as a Career," *Archaeology,* Spring 1961; Gene S. Stuart, National Geographic Society Map of Indians of North America, 1973, with (opposite side) George E. Stuart, North America Before Columbus, 1973; Robert Wauchope, *Lost Tribes & Sunken Continents,* 1962; Gordon R. Willey, *An Introduction to American Archaeology, Volume One,* 1966, *Volume Two,* 1971.

Composition for Discovering Man's Past in the Americas by National Geographic's Phototypographic Division, Carl M. Shrader, Chief; Lawrence F. Ludwig, Assistant Chief. Printed and bound by Fawcett Printing Corp., Rockville, Md. Color separations by Beck Engraving Co., Philadelphia, Pa.; Colorgraphics, Inc., Beltsville, Md.; R. R. Donnelley & Sons, Inc., Chicago, Ill.; Graphic Color Plate, Inc., Stamford, Conn.; Graphic South, Charlotte, N.C.; Progressive Color Corp., Rockville, Md.; and The J. Wm. Reed Co., Alexandria, Va.

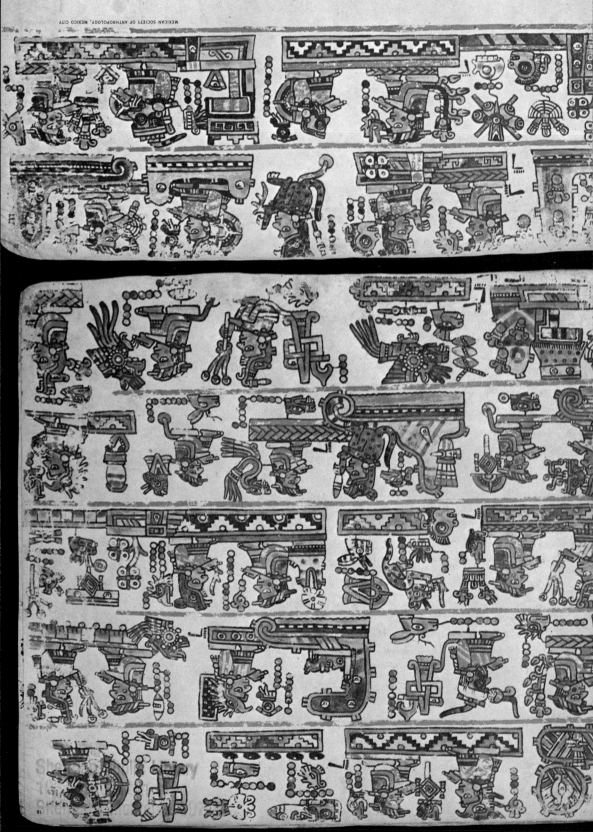

On folded deerskin strips, Mexico's Mixtec Indians recorded year-to-year events and royal genealogies in pictures and glyphs. Such books, like the Codex Bodley reproduced in part here, read from bottom to top. Few of these manuscripts exist. This one, preserved at Oxford University, begins in A.D. 692 and ends abruptly in 1521, when Spain conquered the Mixtecs.